HOW TO DECORATE

Cakes, Desserts & Savouries

JANE ODDIE
&
BRIDGET SARGESON

MEREHURST PRESS
— LONDON —

To Tim and Nicholas

Published 1987 by Merehurst Press
5 Great James Street
London WC1N 3DA

ISBN 0 948075 71 6

Edited by Miren Lopategui
Designed by Roger Daniels
Photographed by Melvin Grey
Typeset by Angel Graphics
Colour separation by Fotographics Ltd, London – Hong Kong
Printed by Henri Proost, Turnhout, Belgium

The Publishers would like to thank Tala Products Limited, P.O.
Box No. 2, Lowdham, Nottinghamshire for their invaluable assistance
throughout the preparation of this book. Icing tubes
featured in this book are from the Tala range.

The Publishers would like to thank the following
for their help and advice:

Joyce Becker

Susan Conder

Nicholas Lodge

China supplied by Chinacraft of London, 499 Oxford Street,
London W1 and branches

The Covent Garden General Store, 111 Long Acre, Covent Garden, London WC2

The Cutlery Shop Limited within Lawleys, 154 Regent Street, London W1

B.R. Mathews & Son, 12 Gipsy Hill, Upper Norwood, London SE19 1NN

David Mellor, 26 James Street, Covent Garden, London WC2E 8PA

David Mellor, 4 Sloane Square, London SW1W 8EE

David Mellor, 66 King Street, Manchester M2 4NP

Elizabeth David Limited, 46 Bourne Street, London SW1W 8JD and
at Covent Garden Kitchen Supplies, 3 North Row, The Market, Covent
Garden, London WC2

Lawleys, 154 Regent Street, London W1

Neal Street East, the Oriental Specialist, 5 Neal Street,
Covent Garden, London WC2

Contents

Introduction

As someone who has to cook in many unfamiliar kitchens and even in huge studios with only a pair of trestle tables to work on, it becomes painfully clear that it is impossible to perform efficiently without the right tools and equipment. I often find myself writing an equipment list as well as a shopping list, as this is of equal importance in getting the finished work right. I so often feel as, say, a woodworker must, that I gain tremendous pleasure from well-designed equipment: for instance, a butter curler that has a comfortably shaped handle which automatically causes you to hold it in such a way as to produce perfect butter curls. Or a clever potato peeler which has light and flexible blades and a handle wide enough to enable a comfortable yet strong grip and yet allow sufficient purchase on the potato, while still not cutting too deep and hence wasting valuable potato, not to mention a major part of the food value which lies just under the skin. In other words a piece of equipment which performs all the tasks it promises to, does them not just well but cleverly, and if it looks and feels balanced, gives a different dimension to cooking, an added subtle pleasure to the art.

In this book I have designed the recipes to suggest a variety of different ideas for decoration and to highlight the uses and advantages of many often disregarded pieces of kitchen equipment. I hope that rather than being a definitive book in its own right, it may encourage innovation by just thinking a little differently about those things we've always taken so much for granted in classic cookery.

Equipment

A selection of equipment used for making and decorating cakes, desserts and savouries.

Cake-making and decorating skills will be greatly improved by having the right equipment. It is worthwhile, therefore, thinking carefully about the sort of equipment you buy. Always choose good quality tins (pans) and utensils which will last. The picture on pages 6-7 shows a selection of tools and equipment that can be used for decorating cakes, desserts and savouries. On the recipes that follow, make sure to use the correct-sized tins as indicated; for unusual-shaped cakes, use the guides on page 12.

Caring for Equipment
Taking good care of your equipment will prolong its life considerably. Particular care should be taken of metal equipment such as icing tubes, syringes and all metal baking tins, which must be thoroughly dried after washing to prevent the formation of rust. Nylon food decorating bags should also be well washed, dried and aired before storing to get rid of any strong food smells and to avoid mildew.

Preparing Baking Tins
For sponge cakes grease the tin lightly with melted fat or oil and then dredge with flour, emptying out any surplus.

For Victoria sandwich cakes, grease the sides of the sandwich tin and line the bottom with a circle of non-stick baking parchment or greased, greaseproof paper.

For rich mixtures and fruit cake, you will need to line the whole tin.

To line a round tin: Cut a strip of baking parchment long enough

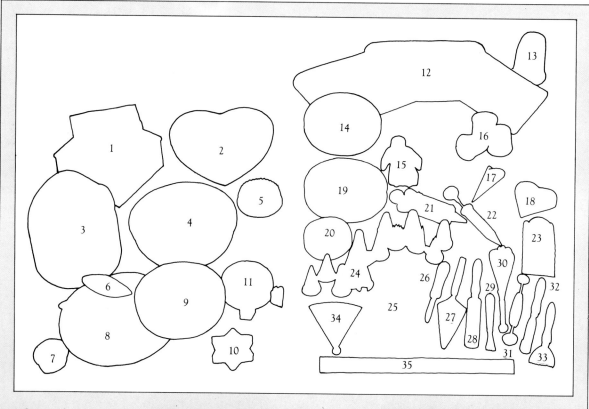

1 Square cake tins	10 Star biscuit cutters	18 Heart biscuit cutters	27 Cake slice
2 Heart cake mould	11 Assorted biscuit (cookie) (aspic) cutters	19 Fluted flan rings	28 Palette knife
3 Round cake tins	12 Tart/patty/biscuit (cookie) tins	20 Pastry cutters	29 Zester
4 Ring tin	13 Sugar/flour dredger	21 Icing syringe	30 Ballon whisk
5 Round fluted biscuit cutters	14 Flan rings	22 Icing pen	31 Melon baller
6 Boat patties	15 Gingerbread (and junior gingerbread)	23 Nutmeg grater	32 Corer
7 Individual patty moulds	cutters	24 Meringue tubes	33 Butter curler
8 Round cooling tray	16 Dariol moulds	25 Icing tubes	34 Icing measure
9 Plain flan ring	17 Cream horn moulds	26 Peeler	35 Icing ruler

to go around the circumference of the tin and about 2.5cm (1in) over, and high enough to come about 5cm (2in) above the tin. Cut a circle to exactly fit the bottom of the tin. Take the long strip of paper and fold the edge up 2.5cm (1in), crease it firmly and snip the folded 2.5cm (1in) with a pair of scissors all the way along the strip. Position the long strip in the tin. Then lay in the circle which will hold the snipped edge of the strip in position. For rich fruit cakes, which need long slow cooking tie a double band of brown paper around the lined baking tin and sit it on a layer of brown paper or newspaper on a baking sheet. (To avoid over-browning of fruit cakes cover the top with a double thickness of greaseproof paper after about 2½ hours of cooking.)

To line an oblong tin: Cut out a piece of greaseproof or non-stick paper about 7.5cm (3in) larger than the size of the tin. Place the tin on the paper and draw around the base with a pencil. Make cuts from each corner to the marked edge. Grease the tin and press the paper on to the base. Press it neatly into the corners, overlapping the cuts in the paper. Grease the paper.

There are many styles of piping tubes available, as shown here. The piped effect of each tube is illustrated on pages 22, 23, 26 and 27.

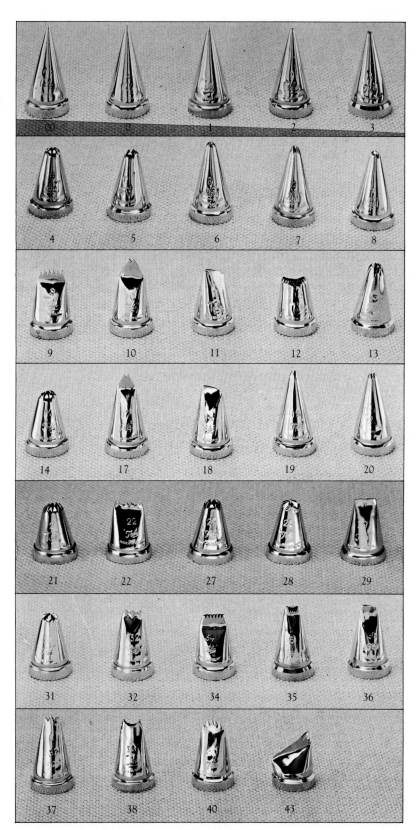

Sponge Cakes

From left to right: Cherry Almond Loaf, Heart's Delight,
Cream and Jam Victoria Sponge, Tipsy Chocolate Sponge,
Carrot and Walnut Cake

Cream and Jam Victoria Sandwich

125g (4oz/½ cup) butter or margarine

125g (4oz/½ cup) caster (superfine) sugar

2 eggs, beaten

125g (4oz/1 cup) self-raising flour

FILLING

315ml (10fl oz/1¼ cups) double (heavy) cream

185-250g (6-8oz) raspberry jam

Cream the fat and sugar until pale and fluffy. Add the egg a little at a time, beating well after each addition. Carefully fold in the flour, using a tablespoon. Using two 18cm (7in) sandwich tins, place half the mixture in each tin, and level with a palette knife. Bake both cakes on the same shelf centre at 190C (375F/gas mark 5) for about 20 minutes or until they are golden and firm to the touch. Remove from the oven and leave to cool. Meanwhile, whip cream until thick, but not too stiff. Warm and sieve the raspberry jam, discarding any pips. Sandwich the cakes with cream and jam, then spread top of cake with cream and trail the jam in patterns, using a dessertspoon.

Heart's Delight

185g (6oz/¾ cup) butter or margarine

185g (6oz/¾ cup) caster (superfine) sugar

Grated rind of 1 lemon

3 eggs, beaten

185g (6oz/1⅓ cups) self-raising flour

DECORATION

A little apricot jam

60g (2oz/⅔ cup) desiccated coconut

Glacé icing, see page 25

A little pink colouring

A little green colouring, or other colouring of your choice

Cream the fat, sugar and lemon rind until pale and fluffy. Add the egg a little at a time, beating well after each addition. Carefully fold in the flour, using a tablespoon. Place the mixture in a greased shallow 254mm (10in) heart-shaped tin (pan) and level with a palette knife. Bake at 190C (375F/gas mark 5) for about 30 minutes until golden. Stand in tin for about 15 minutes then turn out on to a cooling rack, bottom side up, and leave until completely cool. To decorate, warm about 3 tablespoons of apricot jam and sieve it. Add 1 tablespoon of water to the sieved jam and bring to the boil. When the cake is cool, brush the apricot jam on to the sides of the heart and then press the desiccated coconut on to the jam using a palette knife. Make sure that there are no gaps and that there is a slight rim of coconut which will prevent the glacé icing from flowing too far from the top surface of the heart. Colour three-quarters of the glacé icing with pink food colouring, thicken the remaining quarter by adding a little more icing sugar, and colour with green food colouring, or other colour of your choice. Pour the pink icing on to the centre of the cake and spread to the edges of the heart. Spoon the remaining coloured icing into a greaseproof piping bag fitted with a no. 1 writing nozzle and pipe three or four concentric hearts on to the cake, starting from the outside and working in. Then, working very quickly, draw a pointed knife from the outside heart through all the others to the smallest heart at regular intervals, making a scalloped effect. Do not move the cake until the icing is set or the icing may crack.

Unusually-shaped Cakes

For unusually-shaped cakes use the following quantities for each 500ml (approximately 16fl oz) of the tin's capacity.

60g (2oz/¼ cups) butter or margarine

60g (2oz/1¼ cups) caster (superfine) sugar

1 egg, beaten

60g (2oz/1½ cups) self-raising flour

Make the cakes in the usual way and bake at 180C (350F/gas mark 4)

Cherry Almond Loaf

155g (5oz/1¼ cups) self-raising flour

60g (2oz/½ cup) plain (all-purpose) flour

30g (1oz/3 tblsp) cornflour (cornstarch)

250g (8oz/1½ cups) glacé cherries, halved

30g (1oz/3 tblsp) flaked almonds

185g (6oz/¾ cup) butter

185g (6oz/¾ cup) caster (superfine) sugar

3 eggs, beaten

DECORATION

1 extra egg white

30g (1oz/5 tsp) caster (superfine) sugar

Halved glacé cherries

Sift flours together. Mix in cherries and almonds. Cream butter and sugar until pale and fluffy. Add the egg a little at a time, beating well after each addition. Fold in cherry mixture. Place mixture in a lined loaf tin, leaving a slight hollow in the centre of the cake. Bake at 180C (350F/gas mark 4) for 1-1½ hours until well risen and golden brown. Remove from oven but leave in tin. Reduce oven heat to 170C (325F/gas mark 3). To decorate, whisk egg white until stiff and fold in 30g (1oz/5 tblsp) caster sugar. Pile on top of cake and make swirling patterns with the back of a spoon. Return to oven for about 10 minutes until topping is just beginning to brown. Remove cake from tin, cool on a wire rack and carefully peel away paper. Scatter with glacé cherries.

Carrot and Walnut Cake

235ml (7½fl oz/1 cup) corn oil

185g (6oz/1 cup) dark soft brown sugar

3 large eggs

Grated rind of 1 orange

185g (6oz/1⅓ cup) wholemeal flour

1 tsp baking powder

1 tsp grated nutmeg

185g (6oz) carrots, grated

90g (3oz/¾ cup) chopped walnuts

DECORATION

125g (4oz) Greek strained yogurt

60g (2oz/¼ cup) butter

125g (4oz/¾ cup) icing (confectioner's) sifted sugar

Tsp lemon juice

Chopped walnuts

Whisk together the oil, sugar, eggs and orange rind to make a smooth batter. Sift together the flour, baking powder and nutmeg, stir into the batter then add the carrots and walnuts and mix well. Turn into a greased 1-litre (2 pint) ring mould and bake at 180C (350F/gas mark 4) for 35-40 minutes until well risen and firm to the touch. Turn out on to a serving plate and allow to cool. To decorate, make the icing by beating the yogurt and butter together. Beat in the icing (confectioner's) sugar and lemon juice. Put in the refrigerator to thicken slightly. Just before serving, pour the topping over the cake and scatter with chopped walnuts.

Tipsy Chocolate Sponge

45g (1½oz/¼-½ cup) plain (all-purpose) flour

15g (½oz/2 tblsp) cocoa powder

60g (2oz/¼ cup) caster (superfine) sugar

2 eggs

125g (4oz/½ cup) butter

250g (8oz/1¼ cups) icing (confectioner's) sugar, sifted

1-2 tblsp brandy or Cointreau

DECORATION

125g (4oz/1¼ cups) toasted flaked almonds

Icing (confectioner's) sugar

Whisk the sugar and eggs until double in volume and light and fluffy. Sift flour and cocoa together. Fold lightly into egg mixture. Spread evenly into a lined roasting tin. Bake at 220C (425F/gas mark 7) for about 8 minutes. Leave to cool. Make the buttercream by beating the butter until soft. Add sugar and brandy. Beat together well. Cut the sponge widthways into three. Spread the buttercream between the layers of sponge cake. To decorate, spread the remaining buttercream on the sides of the cake and, with a palette knife, press on the toasted almonds. Cut some strips of paper about 12mm (½in) in width and place them diagonally across the cake and then again at right angles to the first strips. Sieve icing sugar on to the top of the cake so that it covers the squares left between the strips of paper. Carefully remove the strips of paper.

Marzipan

Marzipan is an ideal way to cover a rich fruit or firm sponge cake before it is decorated with royal icing or sugarpaste. It prevents any stray cake crumbs from mixing with the icing.

There are two ways of marzipanning a cake. If using royal icing, cut one piece of marzipan to cover the top of the cake and another for the sides, then mould the joins together. Sugarpaste, however, will need a much smoother base, so if you are using this you must cover the top and sides of your cake with one large sheet of marzipan to enable the sugarpaste to lie completely flat on the cake. It is important to bear in mind that the marzipan must never come into contact with flour, otherwise it will ferment.

Marzipanning a cake for royal icing

1 Brush the bottom of the cake with warmed sieved apricot jam and turn over on to marzipan. Cut round with a knife.

2 Measure the circumference and height of the cake, using a piece of string.

3 Brush the sides of the cake with warmed sieved apricot jam.

4 Roll out the remaining marzipan, using the string as a guide. Roll up the marzipan and unroll around the cake.

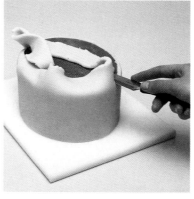

5 Press in place with a jar. Smooth the joins, then use a sharp knife to trim off any excess.

6 Place the board on top of the marzipanned cake and turn over. Leave the cake uncovered in a dry place for at least 48 hours.

Marzipanning a cake for sugarpaste

1 Fill in any holes in the sides or top of the cake with small pieces of marzipan. Smooth to get a level surface.

2 Turn the cake upside down. Brush the top and sides of the cake with warmed sieved apricot jam.

3 Roll out the marzipan. Prevent it from sticking by lifting and rotating it, but do not turn it over.

4 Carefully pick up the marzipan by draping it over the rolling pin.

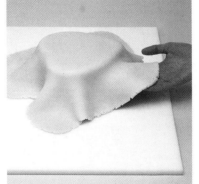

5 Carefully drop the marzipan over the cake, lifting the edges slightly to help it fall without breaking.

6 Using the palms of your hands, work the marzipan into shape. Push up, being careful not to pull down.

7 Use the palms of your hands carefully to smooth over the top and sides of the cake.

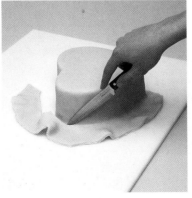

8 Cut off the surplus marzipan level with the bottom of the cake, using a sharp knife.

9 Lift by placing one hand under the cake and drop on to a prepared cake board. Dry for at least 48 hours before icing.

Fruit Cake Recipe

Ingredients (see chart)

Mix together the currants, raisins, sultanas, cherries and candied peel. Add the almonds, together with the finely grated lemon rind, stirring together well. Sift the flour and spices and put to one side in a separate bowl. Beat the butter and sugar together until light and fluffy. Lightly beat the eggs, then add to the creamed mixture a little at a time, also adding some sifted flour to prevent the mixture from curdling. Fold in the remaining flour and mix well, then fold in the dried fruit, stirring until all the ingredients are thoroughly mixed. Turn the mixture into the prepared tin (pan), pressing it down well and smoothing the top with the back

QUANTITIES AND SIZES FOR MAKING FRUIT CAKES

square		15cm (6in)	18cm (7in)	20cm (8in)	23cm (9in)	25.5cm (10in)	28cm (11in)	30.5cm (12in)
round	15cm (6in)	18cm (7in)	20cm (8in)	23cm (9in)	25.5cm (10in)	28cm (11in)	30.5cm (12in)	
currants	250g (8oz/1⅔ cups)	375g (12oz/2⅓ cups)	500g (1lb/3⅓ cups)	685g (1lb 6oz/4 cups)	875g (1lb 12oz/5 cups)	1.25kg (2lb 8oz/6⅔ cups)	1.6kg (3lb 2oz/8⅔ cups)	1.8kg (3lb 12oz/10⅔ cups)
raisins	100g (3½oz/½ cup)	140g (4½oz/¾ cup)	220g (7oz/1⅓ cups)	250g (8oz/1½ cups)	410g (13oz/2½ cups)	440g (14oz/2½ cups)	590g (1lb3oz/3½ cups)	685g (1lb6oz/4 cups)
sultanas	100g (3½oz/½ cup)	140g (4½oz/¾ cup)	220g (7oz/1¼ cups)	250g (8oz/1½ cups)	410g (13oz/2½ cups)	440g (14oz/2½ cups)	590g (1lb3oz/3½ cups)	685g (1lb6oz/4 cups)
glacé cherries (chopped)	60g (2oz/⅓ cup)	90g (3oz/½ cup)	155g (5oz/1 cup)	185g (6oz/1 cup)	280g (9oz/1½ cups)	315g (10oz/1¾ cups)	375g (12oz/2¼ cups)	470g (15oz/2¾ cups)
candied peel	30g (1oz/2tblsp)	60g (2oz/⅓ cup)	90g (3oz/½ cup)	125g (4oz/¾ cup)	155g (5oz/1 cup)	220g (8oz/1¼ cups)	280g (9oz/1½ cups)	315g (10oz/1⅓ cups)
almonds (chopped)	30g (1oz/¼ cup)	60g (2oz/½ cup)	90g (3oz/¾ cup)	125g (4oz/1 cup)	155g (5oz/1⅓ cups)	220g (7oz/2 cups)	280g (9oz/2½ cups)	315g (10oz/2¾ cups)
Lemon rind	a little	a little	¼tsp	½tsp	½tsp	¾tsp	1tsp	1tsp
Plain (all-purpose) flour	185g (6oz/1½ cups)	225g (7½oz/1⅔ cups)	375g (12oz/3 cups)	440g (14oz/3½ cups)	655g (1lb5oz/5¼ cups)	750g (1lb8oz/6 cups)	875g (1lb13oz/1¼ cups)	1.14kg (2lb6oz/9½ cups)
cinnamon	¼tsp	½tsp	½tsp	1tsp	1tsp	2tsp	2½tsp	2½tsp
mixed spice	¼tsp	½tsp	½tsp	1tsp	1tsp	2tsp	2½tsp	2½tsp
butter	155g (5oz/⅔ cup)	185g (6oz/¾ cup)	315g (10oz/1¼ cups)	375g (12oz/1½ cups)	560g (1lb2oz/2¼ cups)	655g (1lb5oz/2⅔ cups)	875g (1lb12oz/3½ cups)	1.02kg (2lb2oz/4¼ cups)
sugar	155g (5oz/⅔ cup)	185g (6oz/¾ cup)	315g (10oz/1½ cups)	375g (12oz/1¾ cups)	560g (1lb2oz/2¾ cups)	655g (1lb5oz/3⅓ cups)	875g (1lb12oz/4 cups)	1.02kg (2lb2oz/5¼ cups)
eggs (large unless otherwise stated)	2 small	3	5	6	9	11	14	17
brandy or sherry	1tblsp	1tblsp	2tblsp	2tblsp	3tblsp	3tblsp	4tblsp	6tblsp
cooking time	2½-3hrs	3hrs	3½hrs	4hrs	6hrs	7hrs	8hrs	8½hrs
weight when cooked	1.02kg 2½lb	1.56kg 3¼lb	2.28kg 4¾lb	2.88kg 6lb	4.32kg 9lb	5.52kg 11½lb	7.08kg 14¾lb	8.16kg 17lb

Note: 500g (1lb) of the above cooked mixture will provide 8-10 portions of cake.

of a metal spoon. Tie a double thickness of brown paper around the outside of the tin. Bake the cake for the specified cooking time (see chart) or until a skewer inserted into the cake comes out clean. Leave the cake in the tin to cool, then turn out, remove the paper and leave until cool on the wire rack. Prick the base of the cake at intervals with the skewer and spoon over the brandy or sherry. Allow to soak in, then wrap the cake and store for up to three months.

Marzipan

This mixture makes approximately 1kg (2lb)

BASIC

250g (8oz/1½ cups) icing (confectioner's) sugar

250g (8oz/1½ cups) caster (superfine) sugar

500g (1lb/3 cups) ground almonds

2 small eggs, lightly beaten

5ml (1 tsp) pure almond essence

Lemon juice

LUXURIOUS

250g (8oz/1½ cups) icing (confectioner's) sugar

250g (8oz/1½ cups) caster (superfine) sugar

500g (1lb/3 cups) ground almonds

2 small eggs, lightly beaten

5ml (1 tsp) pure almond essence

1 tblsp sherry

2 tsp orange flower water

1 tblsp lemon juice

For both recipes sift the icing and caster sugars into a bowl and mix in the ground almonds. Then add the other ingredients and mix to a stiff paste.

Unusually Shaped Fruit Cakes

To make unusual-shaped fruit cakes such as a heart shape, numbers or other novelty cakes, the amount of cake mixture can be calculated from the number of litres (or pints) that the tin will hold. For every half-litre of water that the tin will hold you can use the quantity of mixture listed below, and multiply up as required.

FRUIT CAKE MIXTURE

155g (5oz/1 cup) currants

60g (2oz/⅓ cup) sultanas

60g (2oz/⅓ cup) raisins

45g (1½oz/⅓ cup) glacé cherries, halved

30g (1oz/2 tblsp) chopped mixed peel

100g (3½oz/about 1 cup) plain (all-purpose) flour

¼ tsp mixed spice

90g (3oz/⅓ cup) butter or margarine

90g (3oz/⅓ cup) soft brown or caster (superfine) sugar

1½ eggs

Make the cake in the normal way and bake at 150C (300F/gas mark 1-2).

Wedding Cakes

Good proportions for a three-tier wedding cake would be: 15, 23 and 30.5cm (6, 9 and 12in). For a two tier-cake: 15 and 23cm (6 and 9in), or 18 and 25.5cm (7 and 10in), or 20 and 30.5cm (8 and 12in), would all be suitable.

The tiers should vary in height – the top one being shallower than the bottom. The cake boards should be 5cm (2in) larger than the cake so that there is a rim of 2.5cm (1in) all round when the cake is covered with marzipan and icing, and the bottom layer looks better on a board which is 7.5 to 10cm (3 to 4in) larger than the cake. Wedding cakes are traditionally royal iced but the one in the photograph is iced with sugarpaste, which gives the edges a much softer look.

Fruit Cakes

From left to right: Glacé Fruit Topped Cake, Christening Cake,
Parcel Cake, Two-Tier Wedding Cake.

Two-Tier Wedding Cake

One 15cm (6in) and one 23cm (9in) round fruit cakes, see table on page 16, covered with marzipan and sugarpaste icing, see page 24.

DECORATION

2 iced cake boards

1kg (2lb) royal icing, see page 24

3 white pillars

Ribbons

A little peach food colouring

A small flower vase

Posy of fresh flowers

Waxed paper

Greaseproof paper

Cut two circles of greaseproof paper the same size as the two cakes. Using a compass, on the smaller circle of paper draw a circle slightly larger than the base of the container you will use to hold the fresh flowers. On the larger circle, draw a circle the size of the top cake 15cm (6in). The pillars will stand inside this circle. Place the paper circles on the tops of the cakes and with a pin carefully follow the outlines of the paper and prick the circles on to the cakes. Pipe a white shell ring around the marked pin-pricked circles, then colour some icing peach and pipe a shell border around the base of each cake. To pipe the flowers and leaves, fit a paper piping bag with large petal tube (no. 11), half-fill with white royal icing and on to the waxed paper, pipe lots of blossom-shaped flowers. Then, with a large leaf tube (no. 10), pipe some white leaves of different lengths. You will need to pipe extra leaves to allow for breakages. Leave to set for at least 24 hours. Using a no. 2 writing tube, pipe some white flower stems from the white shell circle cascading down the side of the cake to the base, then repeat several times around both cakes. When the flowers and leaves have set stick them with small dots of white icing to points along and branching off the stems. Using a no. 2 icing tube and peach-coloured icing, pipe some dots in the centres of the blossoms to look like stamens.

Glacé Fruit Topped Cake

One 20cm (8in) fruit cake, see table on page 16

DECORATION

A little apricot glaze

Glacé fruits in a variety of colours

Nuts

A broad strip of coloured crêpe paper

Greaseproof paper

Brush the top of the cake with the apricot glaze. Arrange the fruit and nuts on the cake in rows diagonally, choosing contrasting colours, row by row. Slightly thin the jam by adding a little water or squeeze of lemon juice and brush this thinner glaze carefully over the fruit. Leave to set.

Using pinking shears (if you have them), cut a strip of coloured crêpe paper to tie around the cake. Back this strip with greaseproof paper, so that grease marks will not appear on the crêpe.

Use a thin ribbon to secure the crêpe paper in place and tie with a bow.

Christening Cake

One 20cm (8in) square fruit cake, see table on page 16, covered with marzipan and pale blue royal icing, see page 24

DECORATION

One 25.5cm (10in) cake board and ribbon to surround it

1kg (2lb) royal icing, see page 24

185g (6oz) sugarpaste

Oval icing nail

Waxed paper

Decide upon the design of your cake and draw out the templates accordingly, then transfer the patterns on to the cake top and sides. Using a no.1 or no.2 piping tube and white royal icing, do the trellis work first (see page 29) and then, with a small star tube, pipe a continuous line of stars at the edge of the trellis, along the top of the cake, along the base of the cake and down the four outside corners of the cake. Pipe the birds on to waxed paper, using a no.2 writing tube. Pipe the body of the bird spirally, then press harder to form a blob for the head and draw the tube away quickly to form a beak. Pipe the wings and tail separately. When all are dry, carefully stick on the wings with stiff icing (you may have to support the wings with a piece of foam) and stick on the tail in the same way. To make the cradle, roll out some white sugarpaste, mould it around a lightly greased oval nail. Cut the cradle shape and leave to dry for at least 24 hours. When dry, very carefully remove the cradle from the nail, and roll out some more

white sugarpaste. Cut out a pillow shape to fit the curve of the cradle. Roll a little ball of paste for the head and a small sausage shape for the body and carefully place in cradle. For the eiderdown use a fluted pastry cutter and cut a circle of sugarpaste. Fold over the top quarter of the circle and gently press down (this will be the sheet).

Using a cocktail stick, prick out a pattern to look like quilting on the eiderdown and press the fluted edge of the eiderdown with the cocktail stick held flat, to make indentations like a fringe. Drape the eiderdown over the cradle so that the baby's head is visible. Pipe with a darker blue icing as shown in photograph.

When dry, position the cradle and birds with small blobs of icing. Then tie ribbon around the cake board.

Parcel Cake

One 18cm (7in) square fruit cake, see page 16, covered with marzipan, see page 17

DECORATION

500g (1lb) lilac-coloured sugarpaste icing, see page 24

500g (1lb) white royal icing, see page 24

One 23cm (9in) cake board

1m (3ft) ribbon, about 35cm (1½in) wide

Roll out the sugarpaste until it is large enough to cover the cake. Lift the icing over a rolling pin and lay over the cake. Smooth over top of cake and over two opposite sides, smooth to the base on these sides. On the remaining two sides fold the icing like a parcel, cutting off the surplus all the way round with a sharp knife. Smooth the icing.

Re-roll a little of the icing. Cut out a shape for a label and set it aside to dry. Using a plastic ruler, mark diagonal stripes across the cake and continue the lines down the sides of the cake. Using a no.2 writing tube, pipe solid lines, alternating with dotted lines. Leave to dry.

Measure the ribbon from base of one side of the iced cake, over the top and down the opposite side, turning under at each end. Secure with pins.

Cut the remaining ribbon in half. Fold under one end of each piece and secure to the other two sides of the cake at the base. Draw the raw edges together and carefully tie in a bow. Trim. When the 'label' is dry, pipe 'Happy Birthday' on it in white icing. Place on top of the cake.

Piping

No00
super-fine
writer

No0 very
fine writer

No1 fine writer

No2
medium
writer

No3
thick writer

No4
small border

No5 rope

No6 fine
six star

No7
large
six star

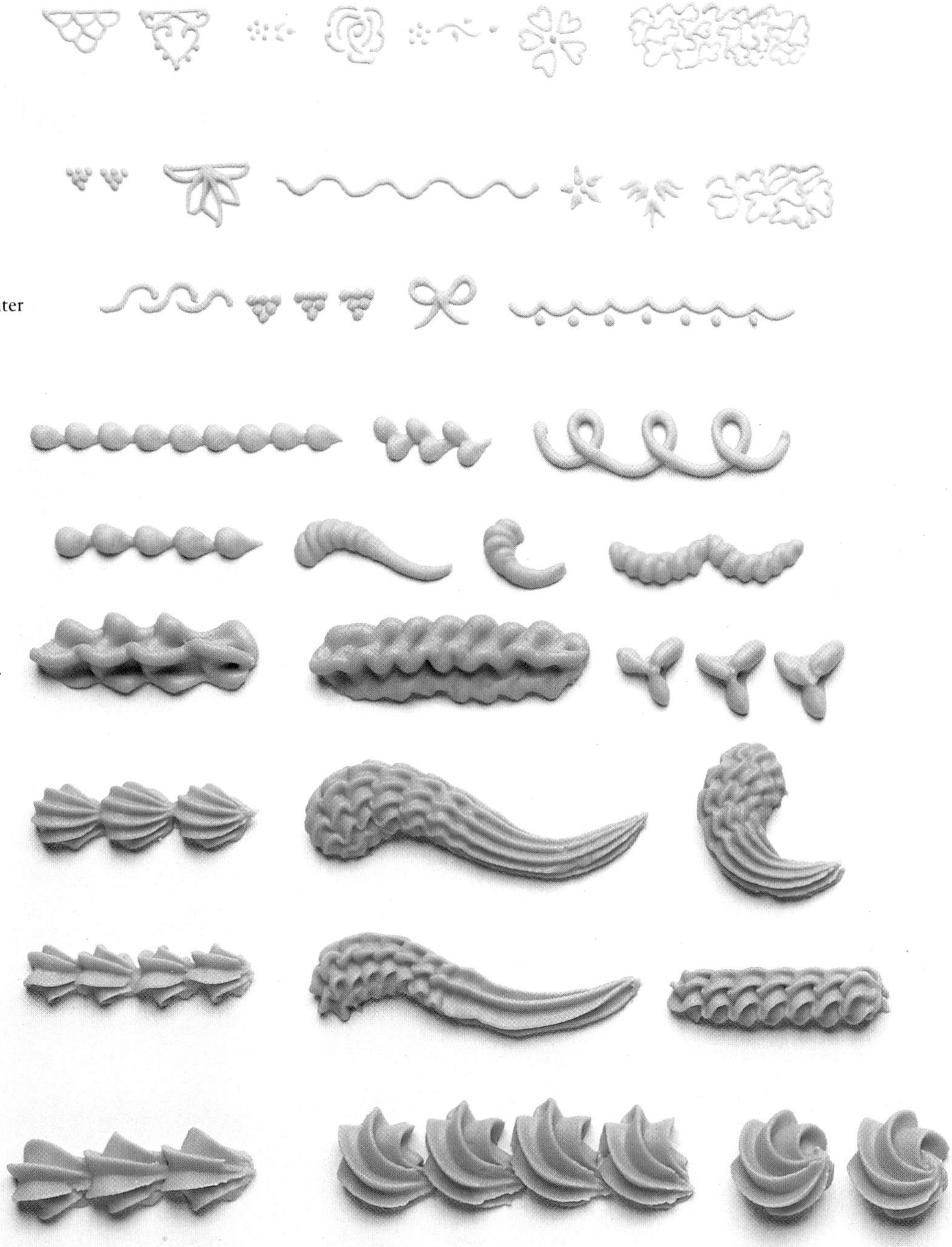

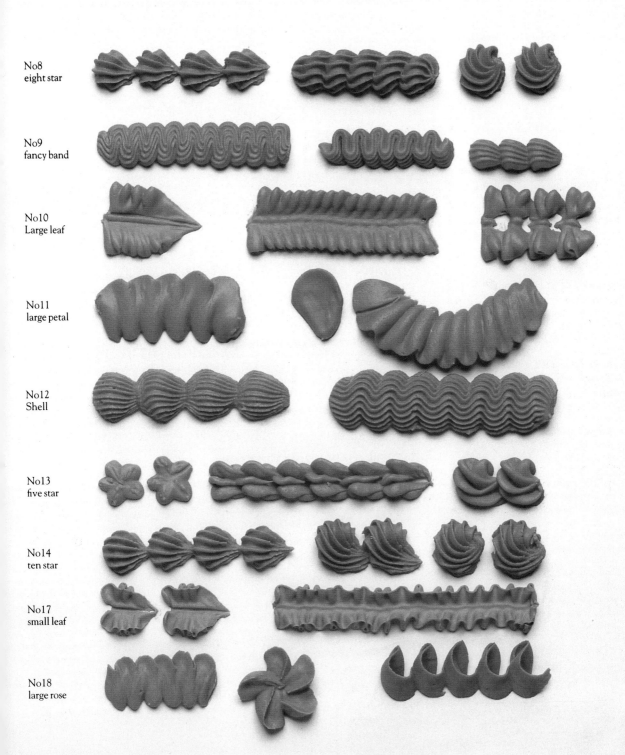

No8
eight star

No9
fancy band

No10
Large leaf

No11
large petal

No12
Shell

No13
five star

No14
ten star

No17
small leaf

No18
large rose

23

Royal icing

4 egg whites

1kg (2lb/6 cups) icing (confectioner's) sugar, sifted twice

15ml (1 tblsp) glycerine (optional)

Put the egg whites in a bowl, being meticulously careful to exclude even the tiniest bit of yolk. Stir lightly just to break up the whites without including too many air bubbles. Add half the icing sugar and stir until well mixed. Using a wooden spoon beat hard for 5-10 minutes until the icing is smooth, glossy and white. Cover the bowl with a damp cloth or large polythene bag for at least 30 minutes to allow the air bubbles to rise to the surface. Gradually stir in the remaining icing sugar. Use as directed. (See page 28 for different consistencies of icing for flat icing, piping etc.)

Quantities of marzipan and royal icing for formal cakes

The quantity of marzipan quoted will give a layer about 4mm (3/16in) thick, and the royal icing will give two coats with enough over for simple decorations.

Covering a cake with royal icing

Royal icing gives a smooth or rough iced surface to a cake. To create rough icing, spread royal icing over the marzipanned cake surface with a palette knife and then pull into peaks with the blade of the knife. A smooth surface is created by applying several layers of royal icing. You will find this much easier if you use a cake turntable.

1 Place the marzipan-covered cake in the centre of a cake board, on a turntable, securing it with dabs of icing. Spread some royal icing over the top of the cake with a palette knife, using a paddling motion.

2 Holding a metal straight edge at 45 degrees to the cake, smoothly draw the edge towards you and across the icing.

3 If the surface is not smooth enough, add more icing and smooth it again with the metal straight edge. Clean the edges of the icing by running a palette knife around the top of the cake, then leave to dry.

4 Spread icing over one side of the cake with a palette knife, using a paddling motion.

5 Smooth the icing down by drawing the metal straight edge or an icing comb over the surface. Ice the opposite side of the cake in the same way.

6 Remove any excess icing with the blade of the palette knife then leave to dry. Ice the other two sides of the cake the following day.

Sugarpaste

This recipe makes a 500g (1lb) mixture and is enough to cover a 20cm (8in) round cake. It can also be used to mould flowers or other decorations and can be coloured.

1 egg white

1 rounded tblsp liquid glucose

500g (1lb/3 cups) icing (confectioner's) sugar, sifted

A little food colouring (optional)

Mix the egg white and glucose together in a basin. Gradually add the icing (confectioner's) sugar to form a stiff paste. Turn on to a board sprinkled with more sifted icing (confectioner's) sugar and knead until smooth. If well wrapped in film and a plastic bag this icing will keep well in the refrigerator for at least six weeks.

If white icing is made you can add colour later by warming the icing (dip in hot water very quickly). Add a few drops of colouring and knead very thoroughly.

Covering a cake with sugarpaste

If using sugarpaste, you don't have to cover the cake with marzipan first. You can apply a thick layer of sugarpaste directly on to the surface of the cake, or you can use a thin layer of marzipan and a thin layer of sugarpaste to get a smoother surface.

1 Place the sugarpaste on a clean, flat surface slightly sprinkled with sifted icing (confectioner's) sugar and knead until soft and pliable.

2 Measure up one side of the cake, across the top and down the other side, then roll out the sugarpaste until it is slightly larger than this measurement. Using a clean cosmetic sponge, cover the surface of the cake with whisky, sherry or boiled water (to help keep the sugarpaste in place).

3 Lift the sugarpaste on to the cake, with the help of the rolling pin, then smooth it into position, taking care not to tear it or trap any air bubbles. Smooth it over the top of the cake first, then work on the sides until it forms a flat covering.

4 Prick any air bubbles with a pin, then rub over the surface of the sugarpaste to smooth it down. Rub a smoother over the surface of the sugarpaste. Trim around the base with a sharp knife to remove any untidy edges.

Glacé icing

This amount will make enough to top a 18cm (7in) cake. Different-flavoured glacé icings can be made by substitution, as in the buttercream recipes (eg. for lemon glacé icing replace the water with 1-2 tblsp lemon juice).

125g (4oz/½ cup) icing (confectioner's) sugar, sifted

1-2 tblsp warm water

A few drops of flavouring essence (optional)

Put the icing sugar into a bowl and gradually add the warm water (and essence if used). Stir thoroughly until smooth. The icing should be thick enough to coat the back of a spoon. Adjust as necessary by adding more sugar to thicken, or water to thin the mixture.
Use at once before a skin forms. For a finer icing the mixture can be warmed, but do not overheat.

Chocolate fudge icing

This recipe will make enough to coat a 20cm (8in) cake.

60g (2oz/¼ cup) butter

2 tblsp cocoa powder, sifted

250g (8oz/1½ cups) icing (confectioner's) sugar, sifted

Melt the butter with the milk. Add the icing sugar and cocoa, beat well until smooth and glossy. Leave until lukewarm but still thin enough to pour, then pour over the cake.

Rich chocolate cream icing

This recipe will make enough to coat the top and sides of a 18cm (7in) cake.

125g (4oz) chocolate

155ml (5fl oz/⅔ cup) double (heavy) cream

Break up chocolate into small pieces and put this with the cream in a basin over hot, but not boiling, water. Stir all the time until the chocolate has melted and the mixture is thick and glossy. Do not overheat. Cool slightly and then pour over the cake as required.

Apricot glaze

This is a versatile friend to the cake decorator. It is used to brush over cakes to attach marzipan. It can also be a glaze for fruit tarts and can be used on cakes before applying toppings such as desiccated coconut, or nuts, or to brush over glacé fruit and nut-topped Christmas cakes. Put 250g (8oz) apricot jam and 2 tblsp water into a saucepan over a low heat and stir until the jam softens. Sieve the mixture and bring to the boil, then simmer gently until it has a coating consistency. After use, any leftover glaze can be saved in a jar and used again.

Piping

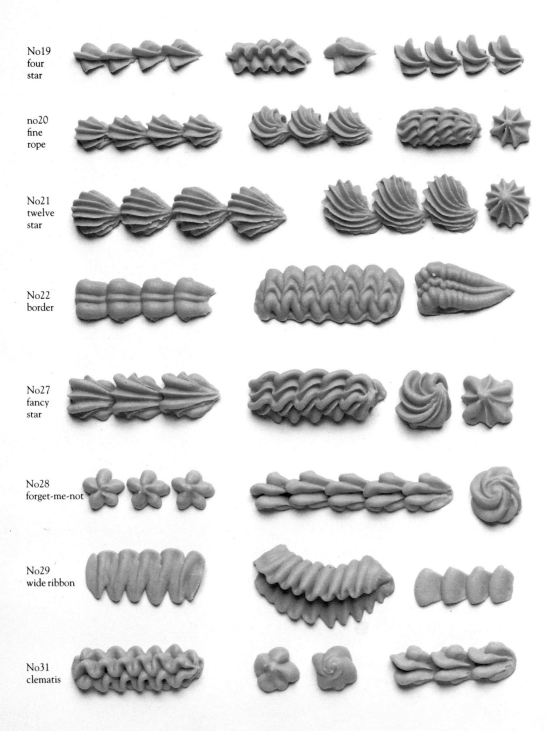

No19
four
star

no20
fine
rope

No21
twelve
star

No22
border

No27
fancy
star

No28
forget-me-not

No29
wide ribbon

No31
clematis

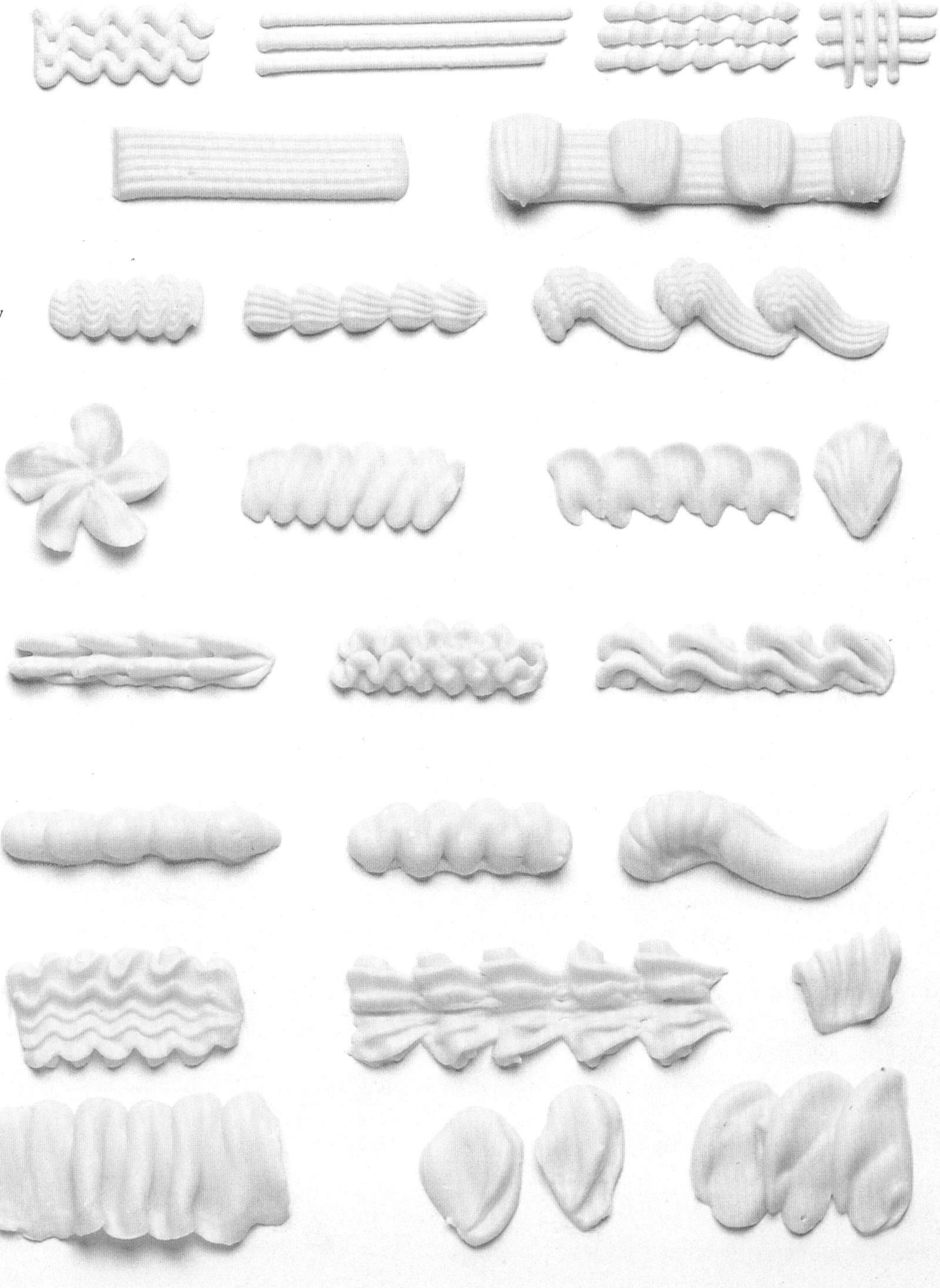

No32
three
thread

No34 wide
ribbed band

No35 narrow
ribbed band

No36
small
rose

No37
fine
fancy
band

No38
narrow
raised
band

No40
fluted
frilled
ribbon

No43
super
rose

As with many other skills, perfect piping is a question of practice. So don't despair if you find it difficult to pipe properly at first. You may find it easier to begin with a nylon piping bag fitted with a large tube and practise piping mashed potato. Once you have experimented with the various nozzle shapes you'll soon build up confidence and be ready to move on from potato to real icing.

The three main types of icing used for piped decoration on cakes are royal icing, buttercream and glacé icing. Royal icing is most often used for more formal piping decoration.

Buttercream is easiest to use when it is freshly made and is soft and at room temperature. If it is too stiff, add a few drops of hot water. It's worth noting, that the heat from your hands can alter the consistency of the icing and make it appear greasy, so it is advisable to put only a small amount into the piping bag at one time, and keep re-filling. You can use buttercream to work designs of shells, stars and rosettes on a cake, but it won't be suitable for fine writing work.

Glacé icing can be used to pipe lines, lacework and writing, but it must be of a stiffer consistency than that used to coat a cake. Beat in more sifted icing (confectioner's) sugar until it reaches the desired thickness.

Royal icing is the most difficult medium to use, as the icing quickly hardens and it's not easy to correct mistakes. It is best used when freshly made. For piping it must be smooth and free from any lumps which can all too easily block the icing tubes. It must be soft enough to force easily through the icing tubes but

firm enough to hold its shape, crisply, once piped. If the icing is too soft it can lose its definition and may not stay in place. Air bubbles in the icing can also spoil the end result. To thin royal icing, stir in a little egg white; to thicken, add a little extra sifted icing (confectioner's) sugar until the desired consistency is achieved. Make sure that the flat iced cake is dry before you begin the piping. As with buttercream, the heat from your hands may affect the consistency of royal

icing, causing it to dry and crack as you pipe it, so use small amounts at a time and re-fill often.

You will need different consistencies of icing for different types of piping. For piped flowers – especially larger ones like roses and pansies – the icing needs to be quite stiff in order to hold its shape, but for fine tube work and writing, it will need to be much thinner so that it will flow, while still holding its shape.

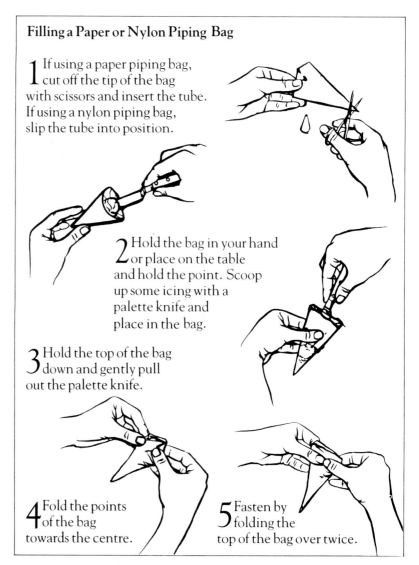

Filling a Paper or Nylon Piping Bag

1 If using a paper piping bag, cut off the tip of the bag with scissors and insert the tube. If using a nylon piping bag, slip the tube into position.

2 Hold the bag in your hand or place on the table and hold the point. Scoop up some icing with a palette knife and place in the bag.

3 Hold the top of the bag down and gently pull out the palette knife.

4 Fold the points of the bag towards the centre.

5 Fasten by folding the top of the bag over twice.

28

Piping equipment

Paper piping bags or small nylon piping bags are easier to manage than a syringe for intricate piping work. Syringes are best for bolder piping, such as rosettes and shells.

To use a syringe: Remove the plunger and, using a small palette knife, fill the cavity to three-quarters of its capacity with icing. Insert the plunger at right angles and secure it, then press the icing to the bottom and attach the appropriate icing tube, using the screw adaptor system. Always work with the number (which is marked on the tube) uppermost as the seam in the metal is underneath and will be hidden.

To pipe straight lines: Attach a plain writing tube, rope tube or other tube of your choice. Place the tip at the point where you mean to begin, then press the plunger. Lift the tube slightly away from the surface and, still squeezing, move the tube steadily in the direction of the line to be piped, keeping the icing flowing evenly. Lower the tip of the tube gently on to the cake where you want the line to end, and release the pressure. Pull the tube away. Never attempt to pipe a line with the tube touching the surface of the cake – this will result in an uneven finish. (You can also use a writing tube for piping dots.)

To pipe stars and shells: Attach a star tube. Hold the syringe in an upright position with the tube quite close to the surface of the cake (about 3mm (⅛in) away), then press the plunger, release the pressure and lift the tube gently away. Still using the star tube but holding it at an angle of 45 degrees, shell patterns can be piped. Squeeze the icing on to the surface, lift the tube slightly, guide it away from you then back towards you and finish down on the surface.

To pipe trellis work: Fit a writing tube into the piping bag, then pipe a series of parallel straight lines in one direction and leave to dry. Now pipe a second row of lines at right angles to the first and leave to dry. You can add a further two or three rows of lines to give a three-dimensional effect, allowing each set to dry between applications. If you make a mistake when piping, the wet line of icing can be removed from the cake with a fine skewer. Scrolls, loops and writing are all techniques that require practice, but they can be easily worked once you have mastered control of the basic piping techniques.

Colouring icing

Food colourings come in three basic forms: powder, paste and liquid. Of these, the powder and paste colourings are best because they have less effect on the consistency of the icing than liquid colourings do.

To colour icing, especially if mixing two or more colours, take just a little of the icing first and experiment. If you like the colour you have created, then add some more of the icing and blend with a palette knife until the colour is thoroughly mixed. In this way, if you have made a colour you don't like, you can then discard it without having wasted the whole lot.

The best way to colour sugarpaste or moulding icing is to add the colour while you are actually making the icing. If, however, you are using commercially produced icing, or need to colour only a part of icing that you've made yourself, a few drops of colouring can be kneaded into the mixture. This may seem a rather lengthy process, but a little perseverance will achieve good, evenly coloured, results.

Templates

In cake-decorating a template is usually a paper pattern that is used as a means of transferring a drawn design on to the top and sides of a cake as a guide for applying decorative elements such as piped flowers, trellis work, frills and so on.

To make and use a template: Carefully measure the top and sides of the cake and cut out shapes in greaseproof paper that exactly match the cake. For a square cake, measure the length and height of just one side of the cake; for a round cake, measure the circumference and height of the side, and cut a long strip to go all the way round. Draw your design on these templates, making sure the flat icing on the cake is quite dry, and then position the templates and transfer the design by pin pricks through the paper to the cake. Remove the paper and decorate as marked making sure that the pin prick marks are completely concealed when the piping is finished. You can use this method to make many different designs, from simple to complex.

Iced Cakes

From left to right: Rich Christmas Cake, Strawberries in a Basket,
Engagement Cake, Rose Celebration Cake.

Rich Christmas Cake

560g (1lb 2oz/1⅓ cups) currants

250g (8oz/1½ cups) raisins

250g (8oz/1½ cups) sultanas

185g (6oz/1 cup) glacé cherries, halved

315g (10oz/2¼ cups) wholemeal flour

½ tsp ground cinnamon

½ tsp mixed spice

315g (10oz/1¼ cups) butter

315g (10oz/1¾ cups) dark brown sugar

Grated rind of ½ lemon

6 eggs, beaten

3 tblsp brandy

DECORATION

A little apricot glaze, see page 25

875g (1lb 12oz) marzipan, see page 17

1kg (2lb) white royal icing, see page 24

Red crêpe paper

Red ribbon

Holly

2 baubles

Mix all the dried fruit with the cherries, flour and spices. Cream the butter, sugar and lemon rind together until light and fluffy. Add the beaten eggs a little at a time. Using a tablespoon, fold in half the fruit and flour, then fold in the rest and add the brandy. Turn the mixture into a lined 20cm (8in) square cake tin (pan), with brown paper tied around the tin (pages 16-17). Spread the mixture evenly and make a dip in the centre, so that when the cake rises the top will be fairly level and not risen in a peak. Stand the cake tin on a layer of newspaper on a baking sheet in the lower part of the oven and bake 150C (300F/gas mark 1-2) for about 4½ hours. After about 2½ hours of cooking cover the top of the cake with a double layer of greaseproof paper to avoid over-browning. When the cake is cooked, leave it to cool in the tin and then turn out on to a wire rack. The cake may be stored wrapped closely in greaseproof paper and foil. To decorate, brush the cake with apricot glaze. Cover with marzipan, then ice with two coats of royal icing (page 24). Using the fancy star icing tube (no. 27), pipe shell borders around the top and bottom borders as shown on page 29. Leave to dry.

Cut a strip of red crepe paper (with pinking shears if you have them) about 5cm (2in) wide by about 86cm (34in) long. Back the crepe paper with greaseproof paper and when the icing is dry wrap the red band around the cake and secure with a pin. The decoration on top of the cake is a ribbon tied in a bow, a sprig of fresh holly (artificial holly could just as well be used) and two coloured glass baubles.

Strawberries in a Basket

ALMOND CAKE

185g (6oz/1⅓ cups) self-raising flour

60g (2oz/½ cup) ground almonds

A pinch of salt

250g (8oz/1 cup) butter

250g (8oz/1½ cup) soft brown sugar

2.5ml (½ tsp) almond essence

4 eggs, beaten

A little milk

DECORATION

A little apricot glaze, see page 25

Marzipan, see page 17

Red powdered food colouring mixed with a little icing (confectioner's) sugar

Royal icing, see page 24, coloured green

White royal icing

Edible silver balls

Mix the flour, almonds and salt. Cream the butter and sugar and almond essence until pale and fluffy. Beat in the eggs a little at a time, beating well between each addition. Fold in the dry ingredients, adding milk if necessary to give a dropping consistency. Place the mixture in a lined 178mm (7in) tin and level the top. Bake for 2-2¼ hours at 170C (325F/gas mark 3). Turn out on to a wire rack and cool. To decorate, brush the top and sides of the cake with apricot glaze. Roll out a circle of marzipan to fit the top of the cake and smooth it into place. Next roll out and cut a strip of marzipan long enough to go all around the sides of the cake and wide enough to project about 20mm (¾in) above the top of the cake. Seal this strip around the cake and leave to harden for at least 24 hours. Mould some marzipan into strawberry shapes. Roll the shapes in the colouring and sugar mix to give a pink dusty coating. Pipe about 25 to 30 calyxes on to some waxed paper using green royal icing and the no. 3 writing tube or the no. 38 raised band tube. Leave to dry completely before attaching one to each strawberry with a dot of fresh green icing. To pipe the 'porcelain', fit a piping bag with the no. 34 ribbed band tube and half fill with white royal icing. Then, working from the base of the cake with the ribbed band of the tube towards you and the plain side touching the cake, make a sweeping movement and pipe a band at about 45° up to the top edge of the marzipan and down again, at 90° from the first band, to the base of the cake. Then halfway between the two bands, make the same movement up to the top of the cake and down to the base. Repeat this all around the cake until the last two bands meet the first. Where the bands cross each other pipe a star and centre with an edible silver ball. When the icing is dry, using a small sharp pointed knife, cut away the marzipan between the icing bands to give a scalloped edge. Pipe white royal icing along the top of the scallops. When dry, place the strawberries in the basket.

Engagement Cake

| 125g (4oz/½ cup) self-raising flour |
| 10ml (2 level tsps) ground ginger |
| 125g (4oz/½ cup) butter |
| 60g (2oz/¼ cup) caster (superfine) sugar |
| 60g (2oz/2 tblsp) honey |
| 2 eggs, beaten |
| 30g (1oz/⅓ cup) crystallized ginger, finely chopped |

DECORATION

| Apricot glaze, see page 25 |
| Sugarpaste, see page 24, coloured pink |
| Royal icing, see page 24 |

Sift flour and ground ginger together. Cream fat, sugar and honey together until light and fluffy. Add the beaten egg a little at a time, beating well, and carefully fold in the flour and ginger mixture, and chopped crystallized ginger. Put the mixture into a greased and base-lined 178mm (7in) heart-shaped tin. Bake at 180C (350F/gas mark 4) for about 45 minutes. Cool on a wire rack. To decorate, cover with apricot glaze and pink-coloured sugarpaste. Crimp the top with a heart-shaped crimper. Pipe the bottom border with white royal icing, using a shell icing tube, and, using a no. 2 writing tube, pipe dots in a lacy pattern. Colour a little sugarpaste a darker pink than that covering the cake. Using a biscuit cutter, cut two heart shapes. Dry on waxed paper. Pipe a white frill around each heart and leave to dry before placing on the cake.

Rose Celebration Cake

1 round cake of your choice covered in pale green royal icing

DECORATION

| Some white and pale pink royal icing, see page 24 |
| Pink ribbon bows |
| Ribbon to band cake board |
| Silk or fresh roses |

With a shell tube, pipe white royal icing to form a shell border at the base of the cake. With a writing tube, pipe scalloped lines over the shell border and on the cake board. With a writing tube, pipe trellis to form the top border. Dry and then over pipe in pale pink royal icing. Add some pink ribbon bows. Using a writing tube, pipe the side design, and finish the cake with ribbon tied around the board and a small bouquet of silk or fresh roses placed on top of the cake.

Icing Flowers

Icing flowers of many types can be modelled using sugarpaste, see page 24, or marzipan. Alternatively they can be piped, using royal icing or buttercream (see pages 24 and 40).

Moulded flowers

Rose

Make a cone with a small piece of icing and press out the base to form a stand. Make a pea-sized ball of icing and flatten between folded clingfilm to make a petal. Carefully wrap the petal around the cone. Repeat in this way until you have five or six petals. Make sure the petals overlap each other. Secure the base of the petals by pressing with a cocktail stick. Once the rose has dried, the base of the cone can be carefully trimmed away.

Daisy

Take a small ball of icing. Pinch one side of it to form a base. Hold the base in one hand and with a finger push in the round side to make a tiny saucer shape, then pinch the edges of the saucer until quite thin, and using small scissors snip these edges to form the petals. Prick holes in the centre of the flower and paint the centre with yellow food colouring. With a fine paintbrush, tint the edges of the petals with pink food colouring.

Arum lily

Attach a 2.5cm (1in) sausage of sugarpaste to a fine wire, making sure that the top end is rounded. Dry, then paint with egg white and dip into demerara sugar (to show the pollen).

Thinly roll out some white sugarpaste and cut into a teardrop shape. Wrap teardrop around the sausage with the rounded end as the base, and seal with a little egg white. The centre shape should be halfway up the petal. Squeeze the point of the petal and draw it backwards slightly. Colour some paste green, roll it out and cut a leaf in the shape of an elongated upside down heart.

Piped flowers

To pipe flowers you will need petal icing tubes (Small, Large or Super, depending on the type and size of flower), a piping bag, an icing nail, some small squares of waxed paper, and, of course, some stiff icing, either royal or buttercream.

Rose

Fix the waxed paper to the nail, using a spot of icing. With the thick end of the tube touching the nail, turn the nail between thumb and finger and pipe a narrow cone for the centre of the rose. Pipe the first petal around this while turning the nail. Then, overlapping slightly, begin piping the next petal but lift the tube, while turning the nail, and touch down again to the nail where the petal is to finish. Continue in this way until you have five or six petals.

For stemmed roses, take a piece of fairly thick gauge wire, fold over the top into a small loop and twist to secure. Pipe a narrow cylinder of icing closely around the loop. Dry, then pipe as described, but let each petal dry before piping the next. Hang upsidedown to dry.

Snowdrop

With white royal icing and a bag fitted with the narrow ribbed band (tube no. 35) pipe a straight band (the trumpet) approximately 2cm (½in) long on to waxed paper, fit the small rose tube and pipe two or three elongated petals to meet overlapping at the top of the ribbed band. Dry, then make the leaves. Take some green icing and a bag fitted with a fine writing tube, and pipe either tiny green dots or a continuous wavy line about 2mm (⅛in) from the bottom of the trumpet. When dry, fix to the cake with a dot of icing and pipe a green stem straight onto the cake.

Violet

Pipe with the 5-star tube (no.13) held at an angle of 45°, so that the three top petals are elongated and the bottom two are shorter.

Pipe a yellow dot in the centre. Then pipe the stems, if required, directly onto the cake.

Narcissus

Pipe a white petal with the tube held flat against the surface of the cake. With the broad side of the tube at the centre of the nail, move the tube out towards the edge of the nail then back to the centre to get a long enough petal. Pipe the second petal at 60° from the first and the third 60° from the second. Pipe the next three petals in the gaps. Then using the no.1 writing tube and yellow icing, pipe the centre, then pipe a spiral to form the trumpet. Finish the edge of the trumpet by painting with a fine brush and deep orange food colouring.

Springtime Cake

one 18cm (7in) or 20cm (8in) round cake of your choice, covered in marzipan and pale green coloured sugarpaste, see page 24

DECORATION

Royal icing tinted violet (for violets)

Royal icing tinted green (for stems and shell border)

Royal icing tinted white (for snowdrops)

Pipe the violets and snowdrops on to waxed or non-stick paper and leave to dry. Mark out with a pin six equidistant 'S' shapes around the top of the cake. Put a little green icing into a piping bag fitted with a writing tube and follow the pinpricks to make six 'S' shapes on top of the cake, branch out from these shapes in places and place a violet at the end of each piped stem, securing with a little icing. Around the lower half of the sides of the cake, pipe different length vertical lines, which will be the stems of more violets. Secure the violets in place using a little of the same coloured icing. Next, with green icing and a fine writing tube, pipe stems for the snowdrops around the top edge or on the curve of the top of the cake, in the shape of an upsidedown tick. Attach the snowdrops with dots of white icing and pipe a shell border around the base of the cake.

Bunch of Roses Cake

1 round cake of your choice covered in marzipan and white sugarpaste, see page 24

DECORATION

Narrow peach-coloured satin ribbon to match colour of roses

Narrow blue satin ribbon to match tissue paper

Some white royal icing for piping, see page 24

A sheet of pale blue tissue paper (approximately 25.5cm (10in) square)

5 or 6 peach-coloured royal icing roses, piped on to stems

A little fresh gypsophilia

Place the ribbons around the middle of the cake; secure with icing and attach small bows. Using the white royal icing, pipe a shell border around the base and top of the cake. Leave to dry. Fold the tissue paper diagonally in half so that you have a triangle. Carefully lay the roses and some gysophilia sprigs on the paper and wrap tissue carefully around them. Secure with a ribbon and place on the top of the cake.

Floral Cake

1 round cake of your choice covered in tangerine sugarpaste, see page 24

DECORATION

A selection of purchased sugar flowers

Some green royal icing for piping flower stems and leaves, see page 24

With a writing tube, pipe the green royal icing in the shape of a bunch of flower stems directly on to the top of the cake and attach each purchased flower with a dot of fresh icing. Then pipe a green vine-like pattern around the edge of the top of the cake. Change to a leaf piping tube and pipe some leaves directly on to the cake among the flowers in the bunch and some more attached to the vine. Attach some more flowers around the base of the cake with some dots of icing.

Anniversary Cake

1 round cake of your choice covered in white sugarpaste, see page 24

DECORATION

Some deep pink and red coloured sugarpaste from which to cut heart shapes

A small and a tiny heart shaped cutter, a large heart shaped cutter and some purchased red and white sugar roses

White royal icing for piping, see page 24

Cut out a large red sugarpaste heart for the top centre of the cake. Cut an equal number of small and tiny hearts to go round the sides of the cake. Allow all hearts to dry and then attach them to the cake with royal icing. Pipe a shell border around the large heart and around the base of the cake.

Buttercream and Chocolate Cakes and Eggs

From left to right: Coffee and Walnut Cake, Easter Eggs, Basket of Roses, Chocolate Hedgehog, Rich Chocolate Cake.

Buttercream can be used to assemble layer cakes when spread with a palette knife, it can be piped into rosettes, flowers, leaves and ropes and has the added advantage of needing no special undercoat, in the way that royal icing needs almond paste. Buttercream is easiest to use when freshly made, soft and at room temperature. However the heat from your hands can alter the consistency of the icing and make it separate and appear to be greasy, so it is wise to put only a small amount into the piping bag at one time and refill as often as necessary.

Basic Buttercream

90g (3oz/⅓ cup) butter
185g (6oz/1 cup) icing (confectioner's) sugar
A little vanilla essence
1-2 tblsp milk or warm water

Cream the butter until soft then gradually beat in the icing sugar essence and milk or water. This recipe will provide enough icing for the top and filling of an 18cm (7in) cake. If you wish to coat the sides and top and fill the cake, increase the quantities to 125g (4oz/½ cup) butter, 250g (8oz/1½ cups) sugar.

Coffee buttercream
Omit the vanilla essence and liquid and flavour with 10ml (2 tsp) instant coffee dissolved in 15-30ml (1-2 tblsp) hot water.

Chocolate buttercream
Flavour with 45g (1½oz) melted chocolate or 15ml (1 tblsp) cocoa powder dissolved in 15-30ml (1-2 tblsp) hot water.

Coffee and Walnut Cake

185g (6oz/¾ cup) butter or margarine
185g (6oz/¾ cup) caster (superfine) sugar
3 eggs, lightly beaten
10ml (2 tsp) instant coffee dissolved in a little hot water
185g (6oz/1⅓ cups) self-raising flour

DECORATION

Coffee buttercream using 185g (6oz/¾ cup) butter and 375g (12oz/2¼ cups) icing (confectioner's) sugar
60g (2oz/½ cup) chopped walnuts
10-12 walnut halves

Cream fat and sugar. Gradually add the beaten egg with the coffee mixture. Fold in the flour. Divide mixture between two base-lined 20cm (8in) sandwich tins and bake at 190C (375F/gas mark 5) for about 25 minutes until golden brown. Turn out on to a wire rack. Leave to cool. To decorate, take about a quarter of the prepared coffee buttercream. Mix in the chopped walnuts. Use this to sandwich together the two cakes. Spread buttercream on top and sides of the cake. Use the serrated side of a decorator's level to make a swirling pattern on top of the cake and stripes on the side. Using a large shell nozzle, pipe around the base of the cake and a border of rosettes around the top. Decorate with walnut halves.

Basket of Roses

An 18cm (7in) or 20cm (8in) round cake of your choice

DECORATION

Buttercream made with 375g (12oz/1½ cups) butter and 750g (1½lb/4½ cups) icing (confectioner's) sugar
Some green, pink and lilac food colouring
Piped buttercream roses, see page 36

Colour one-third of the buttercream green. This is for the basket work and leaves. Add a little extra icing sugar to stiffen the remainder. Divide this into three parts. Leave one part white and colour one part lilac, and the third part pink. Using a writing tube (no. 2 or 3) pipe a vertical line on the side of the cake. With a wide ribbed band tube (no. 34), starting at the top of the cake, pipe a horizontal band beginning 15mm (½in) in front of the vertical line and ending 20mm (¾in) beyond it. Leave a gap the width of the band and pipe another horizontal band. Continue to the base of the cake. Pipe a second vertical line using the writing tube, parallel to the first and 15mm (½in) away. Pipe more horizontal bands using the ribbed tube filling in the gaps. Then pipe the third vertical line 15mm (½in) away from the second and so on. Pipe a scalloped edge around the top. Pipe some leaves on to waxed paper using one of the leaf icing tubes (no. 10 or 17). Fix leaves and roses on to a thick layer of white buttercream on top of the cake.

Rich Chocolate Cake

1 round 18cm (7in) chocolate sponge cake

DECORATION

60-90g (2-3oz) chocolate

A little whipped cream

30g (1oz) milk chocolate

Rich chocolate cream icing, see page 25

Prepare the chocolate crescents by melting the 60-90g (2-3oz) chocolate in a bowl over hot water. Then, in a paper icing bag with the end snipped to represent a no.1 writing tube, pipe an outline in the shape of a crescent or half moon on to waxed paper. Pipe a zigzag of chocolate from one point of the crescent up and down, touching the two curved lines to the other point of the crescent. Allow to set thoroughly. Pour the chocolate icing over the top and sides of the cake, and leave to set. Melt 30g (1oz) milk chocolate over hot water and in a paper piping bag trail chocolate from side to side over the cake. Pipe cream stars around top border and base of the cake, and finish with piped chocolate crescents.

Chocolate Hedgehog

A chocolate sponge layer cake 15cm (6in) or 18cm (7in)

DECORATION

100g (3½oz) chocolate

250g (8oz) sugarpaste, see page 24

Chocolate buttercream, using 125g (4oz/½ cup) butter and 250g (8oz/1½ cups) icing (confectioner's) sugar

3 tiny chocolate drops or edible silver balls

Melt the chocolate. Spread with a palette knife on to a flat surface. Allow to just set, then with a sharp knife held at 45°, shave off long narrow curls of chocolate. Put in the refrigerator until really cold. Cut the cake in two with one part marginally larger than the other. Place the larger piece, cut side down, on to an oval cake board or plate. Cut a corner of the remaining piece of cake to represent the nose. To decorate, roll out the sugarpaste to cover and hold together the body and head, moulding a good nose shape. Trim the icing. Pipe rosettes of chocolate buttercream, close together, starting from the face down the back to the base, round side of face, and work back methodically. Pipe one dot of buttercream for each eye and nose and centre these with a chocolate drop, or an edible silver ball. Work quickly along the back, sticking in long curls of chocolate to represent the spines whilst the buttercream stays soft and receptive.

Easter Eggs

Small Easter eggs

125g (4oz) chocolate

2 or 3 drops of glycerine

Crystallized violets, or rose petals

Mimosa

Decorate purchased Easter eggs with piped chocolate, crystallized violets, rose petals and mimosa. Melt the chocolate and mix in the glycerine. Fill a small piping bag with the mixture and pipe stems and bows directly on to the eggs. Pipe white chocolate flowers on to waxed paper. Leave to dry. Attach chocolate flowers, crystallized violets, rose petals and mimosa to the eggs with dots of melted chocolate.

Piped chocolate designs can be made by placing small templates under waxed paper. Pipe the shape, allow to set, and carefully peel off the waxed paper. Attach to eggs or cakes using a little melted chocolate.

Small Cakes

From left to right: Coffee Cakes, Almond Seedcake Dariols,
Cherry Bon Bons, Coconut Orange Cakes, Gingerbread with Rum
Butter, Strawberry Fairy Cakes, Fruit Buns.

Coffee Cakes

Serves 4-6

A 20cm (8in) square coffee sponge

DECORATION

125g (4oz/1 cup) icing (confectioner's) sugar, well sifted

2 tblsp strong instant coffee

Chocolate vermicelli

Chocolate shapes

To decorate mix the icing sugar, coffee and sufficient boiling water to make a soft mixture. Pour on to the cake. Sprinkle with vermicelli. When the icing has nearly set, cut into squares. Decorate with a chocolate shape.

Cherry Bon Bons

Serves 4-6

60g (2oz/¼ cup) butter

60g (2oz/¼ cup) caster (superfine) sugar

1 egg

90g (3oz/¾ cup) self-raising flour

2 drops almond essence

DECORATION

A few glacé cherries

60g (2oz/⅓ cup) icing (confectioner's) sugar mixed with a little boiling water

Cream the butter and sugar. Beat in the egg, and then the flour and almond essence. Spoon into small cake tins or papers. Bake at 190C (375F/gas mark 5) for 10 minutes. To decorate, place a cherry on top of each cake and spoon over the thin icing.

Almond Seedcake Dariols

Serves 4-6

60g (2oz/¼ cup) butter, softened

60g (2oz/¼ cup) caster (superfine) sugar

1 egg

60g (2oz/½ cup) self-raising flour, sifted

1 tablespoon caraway seeds

DECORATION

60g (2oz) cream cheese

1 tablespoon cream or evaporated milk

A pinch of salt

60g (2oz/⅓ cup) icing (confectioner's) sugar

1 tablespoon crushed butterscotch (use a rolling pin)

125g (4oz/1 cup) flaked almonds, browned under a grill

1 Kiwi fruit, finely sliced

A few frozen redcurrants, thawed

Grease 8-10 dariol moulds, lining the base with a ring of greaseproof paper. Blend the butter and sugar well then mix in the egg, flour and caraway seeds. Bake at 190C (375F/gas mark 5) for 20 minutes, then turn out on to a cooling tray. To decorate, make a crunchy butterscotch frosting by blending the cream cheese, cream, salt and icing sugar together until light and fluffy. Stir in the butterscotch and mix well. Using a small palette knife, spread each cake with butterscotch frosting, then roll in the browned almonds and decorate with fruit.

Coconut Orange Cakes

Serves 4-6

125g (4oz/½ cup) butter

125g (4oz/½ cup) caster (superfine) sugar

2 eggs

155g (5oz/1¼ cups) self-raising flour

155g (5oz/1¼ cups) dessicated coconut

DECORATION

Zest of ½ orange

60g (2oz/¼ cup) butter

185g (6oz/1 cup) icing (confectioner's) sugar

A little orange colouring

Yellow sugar balls

Cream the butter and caster sugar together until well mixed, beat in the eggs and then the flour and coconut. Spoon into small, well-greased cake tins and bake at 190C (375F/gas mark 5) for 20 minutes. Allow to cool for 5 minutes, then remove the cakes from the tins and stand on a cooling tray. To decorate, finely grate the orange zest and blend with the butter and 125g (4oz/¾ cup) icing sugar. Mix until smooth and pipe a small ring around each cake (with a small star nozzle). Sieve the remaining icing sugar into a bowl and add a tiny bit of boiling water until it is a smooth icing consistency (not too wet). Mix in enough colouring to achieve the required tone. Using a teaspoon, flood the centre of each cake. The butter icing will cleverly create a dam. Allow to set and decorate with yellow sugar balls.

Gingerbread with Rum Butter

Serves 4-6

60g (2oz/¼ cup) butter

60g (2oz/⅓ cup) soft brown sugar

1 tsp ground ginger

2 tblsp chopped crystallized ginger

2 tblsp golden (corn) syrup

1 egg

185g (6oz/1½ cups) plain (all-purpose) flour

1 tsp bicarbonate of soda

155ml (5fl oz/⅔ cup) milk

DECORATION

90g (3oz/⅓ cup) unsalted butter

90g (3oz/½ cup) icing (confectioner's) sugar

2-3 tblsp rum

A few walnuts

Put the butter, sugar, ground and crystallized ginger and golden syrup into a saucepan, mix together well, and heat gently, but do not boil. Beat in the egg, and then pour the mixture into the flour, beating well again. Mix the bicarbonate of soda with the milk, pour into the ginger mixture, and mix in thoroughly. Spoon into greased individual cake tins and bake at 190C (375F/gas mark 5) for 15 minutes and turn on to a cake rack. To decorate, cream together butter and sugar and, when the mixture is soft and white, mix in the rum. Using a large star nozzle, pipe a swirl on top of each cake and decorate with a walnut.

Strawberry Fairy Cakes

Serves 4-6

125g (4oz/½ cup) butter

125g (4oz/½ cup) caster (superfine) sugar

2 small eggs

155g (5oz/1¼ cups) self-raising flour

DECORATION

60g (2oz/¼ cup) butter

125g (4oz/1 cup) icing (confectioner's) sugar

3 drops of strawberry flavouring

A little red colouring

A little strawberry jam

Silver balls

A little icing (confectioner's) sugar

Cream the butter and sugar together, then beat in the eggs and flour. Spoon into individual greased cake tins and bake at 190C (375F/gas mark 5) for 15-20 minutes. When they have cooled a little, remove from the tins on to a cooling tray. To decorate, make a strawberry butter icing by creaming the butter, icing sugar, strawberry flavouring and colouring together. When soft and well mixed, spoon into a piping bag with a star nozzle. Using a round cutter, remove the centre of each cake and cut the circle of cake you have removed in half. Spoon a little jam into each cake and then pipe a swirl of pink butter icing into it. Arrange the two half-circles on the icing, in the shape of butterflies' wings. Decorate each cake with a silver ball and dredge with icing sugar.

Fruit Buns

Serves 4-6

125g (4oz/½ cup) butter

125g (4oz/½ cup) caster (superfine) sugar

2 eggs

125g (4oz/1 cup) self-raising flour

60g (2oz/about ⅓ cup) chopped mixed fruit

DECORATION

60g (2oz/¼ cup) butter

125g (4oz/1 cup) icing (confectioner's) sugar

A little green colouring

A little roll-out sugarpaste

Hundreds and thousands

Marzipan fruits

Cream the butter and sugar together, then beat in the eggs and the flour. Stir in the fruit, and spoon the mixture into individual greased tins. Bake at 190C (375F/gas mark 5) for 15-20 minutes, then turn out on to a cooling tray. To decorate, make a butter icing by blending the butter and icing sugar together and mixing until almost white, then colouring with a little green colouring. Fill a piping bag and, using a small star nozzle, pipe a circle of stars around the outsides of the little cakes. Very gently dip into hundred and thousands. Roll out the sugarpaste and, using a small tart cutter, cut into circles. Lay the circles in the middle of the cakes. Place a centre swirl of butter icing and a marzipan fruit in each cake.

Biscuits and Cookies

From left to right: Baby Bakewells, Corn Crisps, Chocolate
Refrigerator Biscuits, Viennese Fingers or Stars, Gingerbread
Men, Shortbread Biscuits.

47

Baby Bakewells

Serves 15-20

125g (4oz) shortcrust pastry, see page 73

1 tblsp apricot jam

65g (2oz/¼ cup) butter

60g (2oz/¼ cup) caster (superfine) sugar

1 egg

60g (2oz/½ cup) ground almonds

DECORATION

A little apricot jam

Small icing flowers

Roll out the pastry and cut into rings with a tart cutter to fit small tart tins (pans). Spoon a very small amount of apricot jam into each tart, then place in a refrigerator to rest. Beat the butter and sugar together and then add the egg and ground almonds and beat well. Spoon a little into each tart and bake at 190C (375F/gas mark 5) for 15 minutes. To decorate, melt a little apricot jam and brush the tarts. Top each tart with a small icing flower.

Corn Crisps

Serves 15-20

125g (4oz/½ cup) margarine

1 tblsp golden (corn) syrup

125g (4oz/¾ cup) brown sugar

60g (2oz/½ cup) self-raising flour

90g (3oz/3 cups) cornflakes, crushed

60g (2oz/⅔ cup) rolled oats

DECORATION

60g (2oz/¼ cup) butter or margarine, softened

125g (4oz/¾ cup) icing (confectioner's) sugar, sifted

1 tblsp strong coffee

A few chopped walnuts

Melt the margarine and syrup together. Mix in the dry ingredients. Spread evenly in a greased swiss (jelly) roll tin. Press down firmly. Bake at 190C (375F/gas mark 5) for 20 minutes. Allow to cool a little, then cut into fingers. To decorate, make the coffee butter icing by blending the butter and icing (confectioner's) sugar together and beating until almost white. Mix in the coffee. Using a rose nozzle, pipe a swirl down each biscuit and sprinkle with nuts.

Chocolate Refrigerator Biscuits

Serves 15-20

125g (4oz/½ cup) butter

45g (1½oz/⅓ cup) cocoa powder

60g (2oz/¼ cup) caster (superfine) sugar

1 heaped tblsp golden (corn) syrup

250g (8oz) broken biscuits

125g (4oz) milk chocolate

2 tblsp evaporated milk or top of the milk

DECORATION

60g (2oz) green marzipan, see page 17

Yellow sugar balls

Melt the butter, cocoa powder, sugar and syrup together in a saucepan, then mix in the broken biscuits and press into a 20cm (8in) square cake tin. Melt the chocolate in a bowl over a saucepan of boiling water and stir in the milk. Pour on top of the cake and place in refrigerator for at least 2 hours before cutting into squares. To decorate, roll the marzipan out on to a board dusted with icing (confectioner's) sugar and cut into shapes to decorate each biscuit, together with the yellow sugar balls.

Viennese Fingers or Stars

Serves 15-20

185g (6oz/¾ cup) margarine

60g (2oz/⅓ cup) icing (confectioner's) sugar

A few drops vanilla essence

185g (6oz/1½ cups) plain (all-purpose) flour

DECORATION

Glacé cherries (optional)

125g (4oz) milk or plain (dark) chocolate

60g (2oz/⅓ cup) icing (confectioner's) sugar

A little pink food colouring

Hundreds and thousands to decorate

Cream the margarine and sugar together, then mix in the vanilla and flour, and refrigerate for ½ hour. Using a large star nozzle, pipe 7.5cm (3in) lengths on to a greased baking sheet – or small stars, which you top with a cherry. Bake at 160C (325F/gas mark 3) for 20 minutes. Allow to cool. To decorate, melt the chocolate in a bowl over a saucepan of boiling water, and make a little pink icing by mixing a small amount of boiling water and a little pink colouring into the sifted icing (confectioner's) sugar. Dip alternate ends of the biscuits into chocolate and icing, and decorate with hundreds and thousands.

Gingerbread Men

Serves 15-20

90g (3oz/¾ cup) ground rice

155g (5oz/1¼ cups) self-raising flour

90g (3oz/⅓ cup) caster (superfine) sugar

2 tsp ground ginger

125g (4oz/½ cup) butter

DECORATE

125g (8oz) marzipan, see page 17

Red and green food colouring

Buttercream, see page 40

Small sweets

Mix the ground rice, flour, sugar and ginger together. Knead in the butter until thoroughly mixed. Roll out on a floured board and cut into people shapes. Place on a greased baking sheet and bake at 160C (325F/gas mark 3) for 30 minutes. Allow to cool. To decorate, colour the marzipan by kneading a little red colouring into half the marzipan, and a little green colouring into the other half. Roll out on a board dusted with icing sugar, and cut out waistcoats, hats and dresses for the gingerbread men and ladies. Using a small star nozzle, decorate each biscuit with buttercream and finish with small sweets.

Shortbread Biscuits

Serves 15-20

280g (9oz/2¼ cups) plain (all-purpose) flour

90g (3oz/⅓ cup) caster (superfine) sugar

185g (6oz/¾ cup) butter

Pinch of salt

DECORATION

250g (8oz) sugarpaste, see page 24, coloured as desired

A little jam

30g (1oz/6 tsp) butter

60g (2oz/⅓ cup) icing (confectioner's) sugar

A little food colouring (optional)

Icing flowers

Yellow sugar balls

Knead together the flour, sugar, butter and salt. Roll out on a floured board and cut into shapes using assorted biscuit cutters. Place on a baking sheet. Collect up all the shortbread scraps and re-roll. Bake at 160C (325F/gas mark 3) for 30 minutes. To decorate, roll out the sugarpaste and cut into assorted shapes using biscuit and aspic cutters. Brush each biscuit with a little melted jam and place the sugarpaste decoration on top. Make the butter icing by mixing together the butter, sugar and colouring to choice. Then, using a small star nozzle, decorate each biscuit with the icing and finish with icing flowers and yellow sugar balls.

Meringues

From left to right: Susie's Gorgeous Pud, Summer Meringue
Swans, Summer Pudding Meringue Gâteau, Sweet Chestnut and
Hazelnut Meringues.

If you have a sympathetic cooker and are prepared to practise, meringues can be easy to make. Useful tips when beating the egg whites are to be especially careful that the bowl and whisk are completely free of any grease, and when you feel that you have whisked the whites to a good peaking consistency, go that little bit further, until the froth not only peaks, but begins to look quite dry. Be as quick as you can when adding the sugar, and remember that even if your oven was a little too hot and the meringues haven't remained as white as they should have, they will still taste delicious.

Susie's Gorgeous Pud

Serves 4-6

125g (4oz/¾ cup) mixed dried fruit

6 tblsp Grand Marnier or other fruity liqueur

2 tblsp caster (superfine) sugar

250g (8fl oz/1 cup) double (heavy) cream

125g (4oz) broken meringues

DECORATION

1 egg white

60g (2oz/¼ cup) caster (superfine) sugar

15g (½oz/3 tblsp) granulated sugar

1 tsp chocolate-flavoured blancmange powder

150ml (5fl oz/⅔ cup) double (heavy) cream

Icing flower (optional)

Roughly chop the fruit and allow to stand in the liqueur and caster sugar for 2-4 hours. Whip the cream until it forms soft peaks. Reserve some fruit to decorate the top. Fold the remaining fruit into the cream, together with the liqueur and the broken meringues. Pile this mixture into a 20cm (8in) flan ring placed on a serving plate. Smooth the mixture flat, then put in the freezer for a minimum of 2 hours, or until required. To decorate, make the chocolate meringues. First brush a baking sheet with oil, then cover with a double thickness of greaseproof paper. Put the egg white in a bowl and whisk until very stiff and standing in peaks. Add the caster (superfine) sugar and whisk until it is shiny and stands in firm peaks. Stir in granulated sugar and chocolate blancmange powder. Pipe several small baby meringues on the baking sheet. Bake at 110C (225F/gas mark ¼) for 1½ hours. Half an hour before serving, remove the gâteau from the freezer and gently remove the flan ring. Whip the 150ml (5fl oz/⅔ cup) cream and, using a star nozzle, use it to decorate the gâteau. Top with the remaining liqueur-soaked fruits and chocolate meringues and, finally, the icing flower.

Summer Meringue Swans

Serves 4-6

2 egg whites

125g (4oz/½ cup) caster (superfine) sugar

30g (1oz/6 tsp) granulated sugar

FILLING

250ml (8fl oz/1 cup) double (heavy) cream

2 tblsp caster (superfine) sugar

250g (8oz) raspberries, hulled

Angelica leaves

Brush two large baking trays with oil. Cover with a double thickness of greaseproof paper. Put the egg whites into a clean bowl and whisk until stiff and forming firm peaks. Add half the caster (superfine) sugar and continue beating until shiny. Quickly add the remaining caster (superfine) sugar and repeat. Fold in the granulated sugar. Put the mixture into a piping bag with a small nozzle and pipe long wing shapes of meringue, and then some neck shapes. Bake at 110C (225F/gas mark ¼) for 1½ hours. To make the filling, whip the cream with the sugar until thick enough to pipe and then assemble the swans on individual plates using piped cream to hold the elements together, and divide the raspberries between them.

Summer Pudding Meringue Gâteau

Serves 4-6

2 egg whites

125g (4oz/½ cup) caster (superfine) sugar

30g (1oz/6 tsp) granulated sugar

DECORATION

125g (4oz) raspberries, hulled and sliced

125g (4oz) strawberries, hulled and sliced

1 orange, peeled and chopped

1 peach, peeled and chopped

1 small bunch grapes, sliced

A little extra caster (superfine) sugar

250ml (8fl oz/1 cup) double (heavy) cream

Brush a large baking tray with oil. Cover with a double thickness of greaseproof paper. Put the egg whites into a clean bowl and whisk until stiff and forming firm peaks. Add half the caster sugar and continue beating until shiny. Quickly add the remaining caster sugar and beat. Fold in the granulated sugar. Using a plain nozzled pipe, pipe two circular platforms to form the top and base of the gâteau. Bake at 110C (225F/gas mark ¼) for 1½ hours. To decorate, arrange the cut-up fruit on the base layer of meringue and sprinkle with sugar. Beat the cream until stiff, and pipe around the fruit. Put the second meringue on top and repeat the procedure.

Sweet Chestnut and Hazelnut Meringues

Serves 4-6

2 egg whites

125g (4oz/½ cup) caster (superfine) sugar

30g (1oz/3 tsp) granulated sugar

60g (2oz/½ cup) finely chopped hazelnuts

FILLING

155ml (5fl oz/⅔ cup) double (heavy) cream

250g (4oz) chestnut purée

1 tblsp caster (superfine) sugar

Brush a large baking tray with oil and cover with a double thickness of greaseproof paper. Put the egg whites into a clean bowl and whisk until stiff and forming firm peaks. Add half the caster (superfine) sugar and continue beating until shiny. Quickly add the remaining sugar and beat. Fold in the granulated sugar together with the hazelnuts and using a plain nozzle pipe small meringues on to the baking sheet. Bake at 110C (225F/gas mark ¼) for 1½ hours. To decorate, whip the cream until it forms soft peaks. Stir in the chestnut purée and sugar. Spoon into the centre of two meringues to form a sandwich. Eat within a day, or the meringues will become soggy.

Desserts Decorated with Cream

From left to right: Bitter Orange Soufflé, Tropical Fruit Trifle, Almond and Grape Gâteau, Strawberry Ice Cream.

Sweet trollies in restaurants should be kept behind a theatrical curtain because of their impact. So often it happens that having finished a perfectly delicious plate of something savoury, and being firmly of the mind that that is it, the waiter brings the sweet trolley and you catch glimpses of strawberries, nutty toffee toppings, beautifully piped cream with meringues perched on the top, fruity sauces with ice-cold soufflés. The combination is usually irresistible.

Piping with Cream

Use a hand-held whisk, balloon whisk or electric mixer to whip double (heavy) or whipping cream until stiff peaks are formed, incorporating as much air as possible. Be careful not to overwhip the cream or it will become buttery and difficult to work with. If the cream is not whipped enough, it will not hold its shape. Using a spoon or spatula, pile the whipped cream into a large piping bag fitted with a large star tube. Push the cream gently down into the bag, making sure there are no large air bubbles, and, working quickly, pipe your chosen shapes, such as rosettes, stars, lines and ropes. Keep your hands cool, or the cream will become greasy. Start piping at the point furthest away from you and work your way back towards yourself, exerting the minimum pressure. If you find it difficult, practice using instant mashed potato on a upturned plate, but you will soon find that you gain confidence to pipe the most elaborate shapes. Once you have completed your decoration, place the dessert or cake in a refrigerator until ready to serve.

Bitter Orange Soufflé

Serves 6-8

3 level tsp gelatine

3 tblsp boiling water

2 large eggs, separated

60g (2oz/¼ cup) caster (superfine) sugar

Juice and finely grated rind of 1 orange

4 kumquats

155ml (5fl oz/⅔ cup) double (heavy) cream

DECORATION

¼ packet orange jelly

155ml (5fl oz/⅔ cup) double (heavy) cream

Sprinkle gelatine on to the water. Stir until dissolved. Make a collar that stands 5cm (2in) above the top of a 500ml (1 pint) soufflé dish using a double sheet of greaseproof paper. Whisk the egg yolks and sugar together in a bowl over a pan of hot water until very thick and pale. Remove bowl from hot water. Continue to whisk until cooled. Finely chop or liquidize 2 of the kumquats. Stir into the mixture together with the orange juice and zest. Add the gelatine. Leave to thicken. Whip cream until light and stiff. Beat egg whites until they form a fine snow. Fold both these into the orange mixture. Pour into the soufflé dish. Refrigerate. Make up orange jelly as directed on the packet, using only half the water. Colour if required. Pour on top of the soufflé. When set, remove the paper with a hot wet knife. Whip the remaining cream. Pipe on to the soufflé. Decorate with chopped kumquats.

Tropical Fruit Trifle

Serves 4-6

1 passion fruit

1 kiwi fruit, peeled

125g (4oz) raspberries, hulled

250g (8oz) can guavas

60g (2oz/½ cup) chopped almonds

4 tblsp apricot brandy

2 tblsp sugar

250ml (8fl oz/1 cup) ready-prepared custard

DECORATION

250ml (8fl oz/1 cup) double (heavy) cream

Angelica

Mix all the fruits, reserving some raspberries for decoration. Add the almonds, brandy and sugar and place in a glass bowl. Pour the custard on top and smooth out. To decorate, whip the cream until stiff and decorate the top of the trifle with the cream, raspberries and angelica.

Almond and Grape Gâteau

Serves 4-6

60g (2oz/¼ cup) butter

3 standard eggs

90g (3oz/⅓ cup) caster (superfine) sugar

90g (3oz/¾ cup) plain (all-purpose) flour, sifted

185g (6oz) green seedless grapes

250ml (8fl oz/1 cup) double (heavy) cream, whipped

125g (4oz/1 cup) flaked almonds, browned

DECORATION

Chocolate leaves

Sugar, to dip

Melt the butter gently over a low heat. Put the eggs into a large bowl and stand over a saucepan of hot water. Whisk for 2 minutes. Add the sugar and continue whisking for a further 8-10 minutes, or until the mixture is light coloured and thick. Remove the bowl from the heat and continue whisking until the egg mixture has cooled. Using a large metal spoon, fold in the butter and the flour, half at a time. Transfer to two greased and lined 18cm (7in) round cake tins (pans) and bake at 180C (350F/gas mark 4) for 25-30 minutes. Leave in the tins for a minute before turning out. When cold, sandwich together with a little cream, grapes and sprinkled sugar. Spread the sides with cream and roll in browned almonds. Decorate with grapes dipped in water and sugar, whipped cream and chocolate leaves.

Strawberry Ice Cream

Serves 4

250ml (8fl oz/1 cup) double (heavy) cream

2 tblsp milk

5 tblsp icing (confectioner's) sugar, sifted

125g (4oz) strawberries, hulled and mashed with a fork

DECORATION

Whipped cream

Extra strawberries

Whip the cream and milk together until stiff. Stir in the sugar and strawberries. Put the bowl into the freezer for 45 minutes then stir in the frozen sides and middle and pour into a tray. Re-freeze for a minimum of 2 hours. Decorate with whipped cream and strawberries.

Fruit Desserts

From left to right: Orange Syllabub Baskets, Strawberry Vol-au-Vents, Fruity Brandy Snaps, Lemon Sherbet.

How lovely it is to indulge yourself in summer and autumn's 'mellow fruitfulness'. In the light of all recent medical knowledge, it is not only a treat, it is a positive way to do your body good, especially as the natural acids in fruits break down fats within the body. Not only are they high in valuable vitamin C, they have lots of natural fibre. Can you think of any more enjoyable way of doing yourself so much good?

Orange Syllabub Baskets

Serves 4-6

CAKE BASKETS

2 large egg whites

125g (4oz/1½ cups) caster (superfine) sugar

140g (4½oz/1½ cups) plain (all purpose) flour

½ tsp vanilla essence

butter, to grease

SYLLABUB AND DECORATION

4 tblsp redcurrant jelly

1 orange

1½-2 tblsp brandy

90g (3oz/⅓ cup) caster (superfine) sugar

250ml (8fl oz/1 cup) double (heavy) cream

125ml (4fl oz/½ cup) sweet white wine

A long rose

Icing (confectioner's) sugar

Make a template for the baskets out of 10cm (4in) deep coffee filter paper. Make curved edges at each side and draw around it on non-stick baking paper. Make a looped pattern in the middle. Turn the paper upside down on the required number of baking sheets and grease with butter. Whisk the egg whites until very stiff, then beat in the sugar and, using a spoon, fold in the flour and vanilla essence. Using a piping bag and plain nozzle, pipe the mixture, following the filigree pattern, and allowing room for the mixture to spread. While the mixture is still warm, remove it from the paper and place it in small bowls so that the baskets cool and harden into the

required shapes. To decorate, melt the jelly and spoon some into each serving plate. Peel the orange zest and squeeze the juice into a measuring jug. Add enough brandy to make the liquid up to 75ml (2½fl oz/⅓ cup). Leave the peel to infuse for at least 6 hours. When ready to serve, whip the cream until stiff and then add the strained juice and wine. Place the cooled baskets on top of the jelly and pipe in the syllabub, using a large star nozzle. Decorate with fine strips of orange zest and icing sugar.

Strawberry Vol-au-Vents

Serves 4-6

250g (8oz) packet frozen puff pastry

2 tblsp syrup

125g (4oz) strawberries

250ml (8fl oz/1 cup) double (heavy) cream

DECORATION

icing (confectioner's) sugar

mint leaves

Roll the puff pastry out 6mm (¼in) thick. Using a heart-shaped cutter, cut out as many hearts as you can so that you end up with an even number. Then, using a slightly smaller heart-shaped cutter, cut a heart shape in the centre of one of each of the pairs of hearts. Stick the two halves together with a little water. Bake at 200C (400F/gas mark 6) for 15 minutes. Melt the syrup and 1 tblsp water together and use to brush the vol-au-vents. Replace in the oven for a further 2-3 minutes. Remove and cool. Beat the cream and use to fill the vol-au-vents with piped cream and sliced strawberries. Decorate with sifted icing sugar and mint leaves.

Fruity Brandy Snaps

Serves 4-6

60g (2oz/¼ cup) butter

60g (2oz/¼ cup) sugar

75g (2oz) golden (corn) syrup

60g (2oz/½ cup) plain (all-purpose) flour

1 tsp ground ginger

2 tsp lemon juice

FILLING

Two 400g (14oz) cans apricot halves

½ melon chopped

2 pieces of stem ginger, chopped

Put the butter, sugar and syrup in a pan. Stand over a low heat until melted. Sift the flour and ginger into the mixture and add the lemon juice. Spoon the mixture on to a greased baking sheet, with a teaspoon. Leave room for the mixture to spread. Bake at 160C (325F/gas mark 3) for 8 minutes. Leave for 1 minute, then lift off the sheet, and while still warm, press into a round-based tart tin (pan). Allow to cool, and place on to the serving plate and fill with apricot, melon and chopped ginger.

Lemon Sherbert

Serves 4-6

3 strips lemon rind

60g (2oz/¼ cup) sugar

2 tblsp golden (corn) syrup or honey

1 tsp gelatine

1 egg white

155ml (5fl oz/⅔ cup) lemon juice

DECORATION

Lemon and lime zest

Heat the lemon rind with 250ml (8fl oz/1 cup) water until boiling. Strain, then add the sugar and boil for 5 minutes. Add the syrup or honey and the gelatine and stir until dissolved. Add the lemon juice and pour into freezing trays. Freeze till part-frozen. Beat the egg white until stiff. Remove the frozen mixture, put into a bowl and beat smooth. Fold in the egg white and finish freezing. Use a melon baller to serve, and decorate with lemon and lime zest.

Sweet Pastries

From left to right: Apricot Confectioner's Pie, Mandarin and
Almond Boats, Baby Lemon Meringue Tarts, Pecan Pie.

It is very difficult to beat a good apple pie, or plum tart, but in these days, when the fashion of the moment expects that added something in presentation, don't forget to use your imagination when decorating the pies – for instance, make an arrangement of shapes cut from pastry trimmings. Using pastry to present a delicate portion in the form of individual tarts and tasty yet dainty boats will not overwhelm the jaded palate. Be unexpected with the details and you will find people not only appreciative of, but also excited by, your inventions.

Sweetened Shortcrust Pastry

125g (4oz/1 cup) plain (all-purpose) flour

60g (2oz/¼ cup) butter

30g (1oz/5 tsp) caster (superfine) sugar

Using your fingertips, rub together the butter and flour until the mixture resembles fine breadcrumbs. Mix in the sugar. Using a round bladed knife, cut in sufficient ice cold water to bind the mixture. Roll out on a floured board.

Apricot Confectioner's Pie

Serves 4-6

125g (4oz) sweetened shortcrust pastry

1 large egg

60g (2oz/¼ cup) caster (superfine) sugar

30g (1oz/3 tblsp) cornflour (cornstarch)

250ml (8fl oz/1 cup) milk

DECORATION

1 can apricots, drained

Real or icing flower (optional)

Roll out the pastry and use to line a (7in) fluted flan ring. Prick the bottom with a fork and line with greaseproof paper. Place baking beans on to this and bake for 15-20 minutes at 200C (400F/gas mark 6). Remove the baking beans and greaseproof paper and leave the flan case to get cold. Make the custard by blending the egg with the cornflour and sugar and gradually add the milk, beating all the time until the mixture is smooth. Pour into a saucepan and bring the mixture slowly to the boil stirring all the time. Boil for 2 minutes to thicken. Allow to cool a little, and then pour into the flan case. Leave to cool completely and then arrange the apricots on the top. Decorate with a flower, if wished.

Mandarin and Almond Boats

Serves 4-6

125g (4oz) sweetened shortcrust pastry

1 small can mandarin oranges

6g (¼oz/2½ tsp) gelatine

60g (2oz/¼ cup) sugar

Zest of 1 orange

60g (2oz) green marzipan, see page 17

Roll the pastry out and use to fill boat moulds. Bake at 200C (400F/gas mark 6) for 10-15 minutes until browned. Drain the juice from the mandarins into a saucepan, and bring to the boil. Remove from the heat and add the gelatine and sugar and stir until dissolved. Arrange the mandarin oranges in the boats with strips of orange zest for added flavour. Roll out the marzipan and cut into small heart shapes – these can also be cut from a slice of orange zest. Use these to decorate the serving dish and the fruit boats. As the mandarin juice begins to set, spoon on top of the fruit.

Baby Lemon Meringue Tarts

Serves 4-6

Sweetened Shortcrust Pastry made with 125g (4oz/1 cup) plain (all-purpose) flour, 60g (2oz/¼ cup) butter and 30g (1oz/5 tsp) caster (superfine) sugar

FILLING

1 large lemon

60g (2oz/¼ cup) sugar

2 tblsp cornflour (cornstarch)

15g (½oz/3 tsp) unsalted butter

2 eggs

125g (4oz/½ cup) caster (superfine) sugar

Using a tart cutter, cut the pastry into rings and press gently into tart tins (pans). Grate the zest of the lemon and put in a saucepan with the sugar and 250ml (8fl oz/1 cup) water, bring to the boil. Squeeze the lemon and blend the juice with the cornflour. Pour into the saucepan, add the butter, and beat well until smooth and shiny. Remove from the heat. Separate the eggs and beat the yolks into the slightly cooled mixture. Spoon into tart cases. Beat the egg whites until firm and stiff, beat in half the caster sugar and fold in the remaining. Put into a piping bag with a small star nozzle and pipe the meringue on top of the tarts. Bake at 180C (350F/gas mark 4) for 30 minutes.

Pecan Pie

Serves 4-6

125g (4oz) sweetened shortcrust pastry

4 tblsp fresh white breadcrumbs

4 tblsp golden (corn) syrup

30g (1oz/6tsp) butter

DECORATION

Pecan nuts (shelled)

2 tblsp maple syrup

Roll out the pastry and use to line a 18cm (7in) fluted flan ring on a baking sheet. Put the breadcrumbs, golden syrup and butter in a saucepan and warm gently. Mix together and pour into the flan. To decorate, arrange the pecan nuts on the top and bake at 190C (375F/gas mark 5) for 25-30 minutes. Remove the flan ring while the pie is still hot and the syrup is not yet sticky. Put the pie on to a serving plate and spoon the maple syrup over the top.

Choux and Filo Pastry Desserts

From left to right: Almond Ring with Brandy Cream, Individual Gâteaux St Honoré, Chocolate Éclairs with Mocha Cream, Lemon and Coconut Crisps.

Choux pastry is surprisingly easy to make and very effective and tasty. It is also very easy to handle and to pipe. The secret is to beat the mixture really well, and eat the choux fresh. Today many pastries are so conveniently available in the chiller or freezer cabinet in the supermarket. A good example is filo pastry – a difficult pastry to achieve at home. This is a particularly versatile pastry because of its light and delicate texture, and is exciting because it is still unusual to most people.

Almond Ring with Brandy Cream

Serves 6

75g (2½oz/about ¾ cup) plain (all-purpose) flour

A pinch of salt

Water

60g (2oz/¼ cup) butter

2 eggs, well beaten

Maple syrup

60g (2oz/½ cup) flaked almonds

FILLING AND DECORATION

155ml (5fl oz/⅔ cup) double (heavy) cream

2 tblsp brandy

1 tblsp sugar

1 orange

Sift the flour and salt. Put 155ml (5fl oz/⅔ cup) water and the butter in a saucepan and bring to the boil. When boiling fast, remove from the heat and pour in the flour. Using a wooden spoon, beat well until the mixture forms a soft ball, reheating if necessary. Allow to cool a little before beating in the eggs. Using a large nozzle, pipe two thick rings onto two greased baking sheets. Bake at 200C (400F/gas mark 6) for the first 10 minutes then turn the heat down to 180C (350F/gas mark 4) for a further 25 minutes. Brush the rings with maple syrup and sprinkle with almonds 15 minutes before the end of the cooking time. To decorate, when the rings are cool, sandwich together with whipped cream, brandy and sugar. Decorate with orange slices and small flowers cut from the zest.

Individual Gâteaux St Honoré

Serves 4

PASTRY

125g (4oz/1 cup) plain (all-purpose) flour

salt

30g (1oz/6tsp) unsalted butter

30g (1oz/6tsp) lard

1 tblsp caster (superfine) sugar

CHOUX PASTRY

30g (1oz/6tsp) butter

60g (2oz/½ cup) plain (all-purpose) flour

1 egg

FILLING

250ml (8fl oz/1 cup) double (heavy) cream

250ml (8fl oz/1 cup) single (light) cream

60g (2oz/⅓ cup) vanilla sugar

4 apricot halves

125g (4oz) strawberries

icing (confectioner's) sugar, to dust

Rub the butter and lard into the flour and salt. When the mixture resembles fine breadcrumbs, stir in the sugar, and sufficient water to bind the mixture together. Roll out and cut into four small rounds with a plain cutter. Place on two greased baking trays. Make the choux pastry by bringing the butter and 155ml (5fl oz/⅔ cup) water to a rolling boil and beating in the flour off the heat. Allow to cool a little and beat in the egg. Put this mixture into a piping bag with a small plain nozzle and use to pipe a ring of small buns around the outside of the pastry circles. Bake at 200C (400F/gas mark 6) for 15-20 minutes. Remove from the oven, dredge with icing sugar and cool. To make the filling, whisk the two creams with the vanilla sugar and fill the gateaux with cream using a piping bag with a plain nozzle. Fill with apricots and strawberries, and dust with icing sugar.

Chocolate Éclairs with Mocha Cream

Serves 4-6

| 75g (2½oz/about ¾ cup) plain (all-purpose) flour |
| A pinch of salt |
| 60g (2oz/¼ cup) butter |
| 2 standard eggs, well beaten |
| FILLING AND DECORATION |
| 250g (8oz) milk chocolate |
| 250ml (8fl oz/1 cup) double (heavy) cream |
| 1 tblsp sugar |
| 1 tblsp Camp coffee (or strong instant coffee) |

Sift the flour and salt. Put 155ml (5fl oz/⅔ cup) water and butter in a saucepan and bring to the boil. When boiling fast, remove from the heat and pour in the flour. Using a wooden spoon, beat well until the mixture forms a soft ball, reheating if necessary. Allow to cool a little before beating in the eggs. Put into a piping bag with a plain nozzle and pipe small buns on to a greased baking sheet. Bake at 200C (400F/ gas mark 6) for the first 10 minutes, then reduce the heat to 180C (350F/ gas mark 4) for a further 20-25 minutes. To decorate, melt the chocolate in a bowl over boiling water. Dip each éclair into the chocolate and allow to cool. Beat the cream, sugar and coffee together and fill a piping bag with a small plain nozzle, push the end through the side of the éclair and fill the centre with the mocha cream.

Lemon and Coconut Crisps

Serves 4-6

| 250g (8oz) packet frozen filo pastry |
| Lemon curd, to fill |
| 125g (4oz/2½ cups) shredded coconut |

With a round cutter, cut lots of round shapes from the filo pastry. Press two circles into each tart tin (pan). Put a teaspoonful of lemon curd into each tart, and bake at 190C (375F/gas mark 5) for 10-15 minutes. Toast the coconut and sprinkle on top of the crisps.

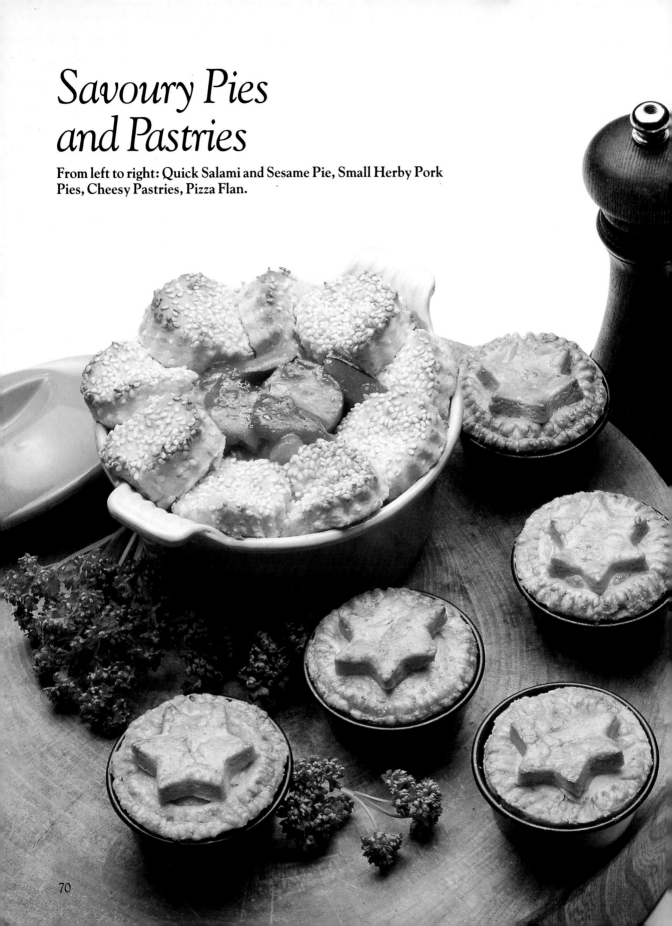

Savoury Pies and Pastries

From left to right: Quick Salami and Sesame Pie, Small Herby Pork Pies, Cheesy Pastries, Pizza Flan.

Pies and Pastries are probably the original convenience foods, the egg being a more notable exception. Pies were a clever design of hardworking housewives who had to send their men off to their work with a good meal tied up in their 'kerchief. So need being, 'the Mother of invention', these very practical ladies designed Cornish pasties, steak and kidney pies, pork pies and the like, to do a good nourishing job for them. There are a lot of very profitable food companies still saluting these dear ladies of centuries ago. We in the culinary line just bend the rules a little and make our pastries and pies a little different and more in tune with modern living, adding exciting flavours to our pastries, and unusual vegetable and meat combinations to tickle the palate.

Quick Salami and Sesame Pie

Serves 4

125g (4oz) small mushrooms

1 onion, peeled and chopped

15g (16oz) can diced tomatoes

1 small red pepper, chopped

1 clove garlic, crushed

SCONE TOPPING

250g (8oz/2 cups) self-raising flour

½ tsp salt

125g (4oz/½ cup) butter or margarine

4 tblsp milk

Extra milk, to brush

2 tblsp sesame seeds

Mix the mushrooms, onion, tomatoes, red pepper and garlic. Spoon equally between four dishes. Make the scone topping by mixing the flour and salt, and rubbing in the butter. Mix in the milk to make a soft dough. Roll out on a floured board until 12mm (½in) thick. Cut into fluted rings. Brush with milk and dip in sesame seeds and arrange around the dishes. Bake at 200C (400F/gas mark 6) for 40 minutes.

Small Herby Pork Pies

Serves 6

375g (12oz/3 cups) plain (all-purpose) flour

½ tsp salt

2 tsp dried sage

1 tsp dried onion

Egg yolk

4 tblsp milk

30g (1oz/6 tsp) butter

90g (3oz/⅓ cup) lard

1 egg to glaze

FILLING

500g (1lb) minced pork

1 onion, grated

2 tblsp plain (all-purpose) flour

Water

Salt and pepper

Sift the flour and salt into a bowl. Mix in the sage and onion. Beat the egg yolk and milk together and pour into the well. Mix butter and lard with 4 tblsp water and bring to a boil. Pour into the flour and egg and mix well with a wooden spoon. Turn out on to a floured board and divide into six. Mix the pork, onion, flour and seasoning with 125ml (4fl oz/½ cup) water. Mould two-thirds of each of the pastry portions into a small pie tin (pan). Spoon in the pork filling and roll the remaining pastry to top the pie. Use any trimmings to cut shapes as pastry trim. Brush with egg and bake at 200C (400F/gas mark 6) for 15 minutes, then reduce to 180C (350F/gas mark 4).

Cheesy Pastries

Serves 4-6

125g (4oz/1 cup) plain (all-purpose) flour

60g (2oz/¼ cup) butter

30g (1oz/½ cup) bran

60g (2oz/¼ cup) grated Cheddar cheese

Parmesan, to finish

Rub the flour, butter and bran together, then stir in the grated Cheddar. Roll out on floured board. Cut into interesting shapes and bake at 200C (400F/gas mark 6) for 10-15 minutes until browned. Sprinkle with Parmesan and serve warm.

Pizza Flan

Serves 4-6

125g (4oz) shortcrust pastry

One 420g (14oz) can chopped tomatoes

1 small onion, peeled and diced

125 (4oz/1 cup) Cheddar cheese, grated

2 eggs, beaten

1 tsp oregano

One 60g (2oz) can anchovies

60g (2oz/⅓ cup) olives

Roll out the pastry and use to fill a fluted flan case. Mix the tomatoes, onion and cheese with the egg and oregano and pour into the flan case. Bake at 200C (400F/gas mark 6) for 20 minutes. Take out of the oven and arrange the anchovies and olives on top. Replace in the oven for a further 15 minutes.

Shortcrust Pastry

125g (4oz/1 cup) plain (all-purpose) flour

60g (2oz/¼ cup) butter or margarine

Using your fingertips, rub together the butter and flour until the mixture resembles fine breadcrumbs. Using a round bladed knife, cut in sufficient ice cold water to bind the mixture. Roll out on a floured board.

Wholemeal Pastry
Follow the recipe for Shortcrust Pastry, but use wholemeal flour instead of plain (all-purpose) flour. Add a little extra ice cold water to bind the mixture.

Cheese Pastry
Follow the recipe for Shortcrust Pastry, but add 60g (2oz) grated Cheddar or other hard cheese before mixing in the water.

Savoury Dishes

**From left to right: Celery Boats, Curry and Cream Cheese Dariols,
Crispy Chinese Tarts, Fisherman's Pies.**

Piped potato can give a very professional finish to a dish. If you bake it or grill it you have an added dimension of two completely different textures. It is possible to take this a step further and have cheesy potato on your Shepherd's Pie, or garlic and parsley potato around a chicken filling. Try the recipe for Duchesse Potatoes, not shown in the picture, as an attractive garnish for savoury dishes. It is very tasty if you boil swede, parsnip, potato and carrot together, mash them and then pipe them as a topping to a cheese and lentil base. Try combining different cheeses, as I have here in Celery Boats. This combination can also be delicious piped into pear halves and sprinkled with chopped walnuts, or used as a sandwich filling with cress and shredded fennel. The old days when 'Starters' began a meal are over. Today we happily admit to the sneaky feeling that 'two starters' could be much more exciting than many traditional courses. The subtle play of flavours and textures is somehow more important than a good filling meal – though this, of course, has its place as well on a cold winter's day.

Celery Boats

Serves 6-8

1 head celery, well washed and cut into 5cm (2in) pieces
125g (4oz) cream cheese
60g (2oz) Stilton cheese
4 tblsp plain yogurt
2 spring onions (scallions), roughly chopped

Blend the cheeses, yogurt and onions together to form a cream suitable for piping. Spoon into a piping bag with a large star nozzle and pipe the mixture into the celery pieces. Chill before serving.

Curry and Cream Cheese Dariols

Serves 4-6

15g (½oz/5 tsp) gelatine
250ml (8fl oz/1 cup) consommé
125g (4oz) red lumpfish
Sprigs of fresh herbs
250g (8oz) cream cheese
1 tsp curry paste
½ tblsp apricot jam

Sprinkle the gelatine over a little boiling water and stir until it is completely dissolved. Add 125ml (4fl oz/½ cup) of the consommé and stir well. Mix the red lumpfish with the remaining consommé. Put a small sprig of fresh herbs into the base of each of the six dariol moulds and divide the lumpfish and consommé mixture equally between the moulds. Chill in the refrigerator until set. Blend the consommé mixture with the cream cheese, curry paste and apricot jam. Pour on top of the set layer of lumpfish mixture and put in the refrigerator to set. Decorate the dish with fresh salad sprigs.

Crispy Chinese Tarts

Serves 6-8

12 ready sliced pieces of white bread, crusts removed

A little butter

125g (4oz) taramasalata

1 small onion, peeled and sliced

1 egg

155ml (5fl oz/⅔ cup) milk

2 spring green leaves

shallow fat, to fry

12 olives

Butter the bread and press the buttered side down into small tart tins. Mix the taramasalata, onion, egg and milk together and pour into each bread tart. Bake at 200C (400F/gas mark 6) for 5-10 minutes until they are brown and the centre is set. Shred the leaves from the spring greens very finely and fry in hot shallow fat. Drain well and divide between the tarts. Top with an olive and serve warm.

Fisherman's Pies

Serves 4

1kg (2lb) potatoes, peeled, boiled and mashed

60g (2oz/¼ cup) butter

1 egg

FILLING

60g (2oz/¼ cup) butter

2 spring onions (scallions) chopped

2 sticks celery, chopped

60g (2oz/½ cup) plain (all-purpose) flour

250ml (8fl oz/1 cup) milk

125g (4oz) shelled prawns

Juice of ½ lemon

Seasoning

Two 125g (4oz) cans sardines in oil

Mix the potato with the butter and egg and fill a piping bag fitted with a large star piping nozzle. Pipe a border around four individual heatproof dishes. For the filling, melt the butter and toss the chopped spring onions and celery in it. Stir in the flour and allow to cook a little, then add the milk very gradually and keep stirring until the mixture thickens and boils. Add the prawns and lemon juice and season to taste. Pour the mixture into each potato case and top with one or two sardines. Bake at 200C (400F/gas mark 6) for 10 minutes, or under a hot grill until browned.

Duchesse Potatoes

Serves 4

750g (1½lb) potatoes, peeled, boiled and mashed

60g (2oz) butter

1 egg, beaten

Salt and pepper

Grated nutmeg

Mix the potato with the butter, egg, seasoning and nutmeg. Cool. Grease a baking sheet. Pile the potato mixture into a large piping bag fitted with a star tube. Pipe on to the baking sheet and bake at 200C (400F/gas mark 6) for 20 to 25 minutes until golden brown. Use to garnish savoury dishes.

Canapés

From left to right: Pumpernickle Sandwiches, Parma and Melon
Sticks, Seafood Boats, Tuna Fish Horns, Cheese and Celery
Samosas, Prawn Toasts.

Pumpernickle Sandwiches

Serves 6-8

Pumpernickle bread

Mayonnaise

A choice of hard-boiled eggs, stuffed olives, or cheese slices

Cut the pumpernickle and cheese with shaped cutters. Spread with mayonnaise and fill with cheese, egg, or whatever you have in your cupboard.

Parma and Melon Sticks

Serves 6-8

1 melon, seeded

125g (4oz) Parma ham

Using a melon baller, cut as many balls of melon as you can. Roll the ham and alternate with the melon balls on cocktail sticks.

Seafood Boats

Serves 6-8

250g (8oz) shortcrust pastry, see page 72

125g (4oz) black lumpfish

125g (4oz) red lumpfish

Fennel and cream cheese

Roll the pastry to fill boat moulds. Bake at 200C (400F/gas mark 6) for 10 minutes. Cool and fill with alternate strips of lumpfish. Decorate with fennel and piped cream cheese.

Tuna Fish Horns

Serves 6-8

240g (8oz) packet frozen puff pastry, thawed

1 small egg, beaten

One 240g (8oz) can tuna fish

250g (8oz) cream cheese

½ clove garlic, crushed

DECORATION

chopped parsley

Chopped walnuts

Roll out the pastry and cut into 12mm (½in) strips. Roll around a cream horn mould to halfway up. Glaze with beaten egg and bake at 200C (400F/gas mark 6) for 15 minutes. When cooled remove the horn tins. Mash the tuna, cream cheese and garlic together. Pipe into the pastries and dip either in parsley or walnuts.

Cheese and Celery Samosas

Serves 6-8

240g (8oz) packet frozen puff pastry, thawed

125g (4oz/1 cup) finely grated Cheddar cheese

2 sticks celery, finely chopped

2 tblsp chutney

Fat, to fry

Roll the puff pastry out until 12mm (½in) thick, cut with 5cm (2in) fluted cutters. Mix the cheese, celery and chutney, and spoon into the pastry circles. Wet the edges and press closed. Chill in the refrigerator for 30 minutes, then fry gently in deep fat. Drain and serve.

Prawn Toasts

Serves 6-8

½ loaf thick sliced white bread

2 rashers belly pork, rind removed

125g (4oz) frozen shelled prawns, thawed

60g (2oz/¼ cup) white breadcrumbs

1 egg

½ onion, peeled and chopped

60g (2oz/¼ cup) sesame seeds

Deep fat, to fry

Cream cheese and fresh, chopped herbs

Grind the pork, prawns, breadcrumbs, egg and onion together in a liquidizer. Spread on top of the bread and cut off the crusts, and fry face down in hot fat, turning frequently for 10 minutes. Scatter with sesame seeds. Cut into fingers, or other shapes, as preferred. Decorate with piped cream cheese and sprinkle with chopped herbs.